First World War
and Army of Occupation
War Diary
France, Belgium and Germany

2 DIVISION
Divisional Troops
Royal Army Medical Corps
4 Field Ambulance
1 April 1915 - 30 April 1915

WO95/1336/4

The Naval & Military Press Ltd
www.nmarchive.com
Published in association with The National Archives

Published by

The Naval & Military Press Ltd

Unit 10 Ridgewood Industrial Park,

Uckfield, East Sussex,

TN22 5QE England

Tel: +44 (0) 1825 749494

www.naval-military-press.com

www.nmarchive.com

This diary has been reprinted in facsimile from the original. Any imperfections are inevitably reproduced and the quality may fall short of modern type and cartographic standards.

© Crown Copyright
Images reproduced by permission of The National Archives, London, England, 2015.

Contents

Document type	Place/Title	Date From	Date To
Heading	April 1915		
War Diary	Bethune	01/04/1915	01/04/1915
Miscellaneous	No.4 Field Ambulance	01/04/1915	01/04/1915
Miscellaneous	No.4 Field Ambulance Evacuation Return 3pm	01/04/1915	01/04/1915
War Diary	Bethune	02/04/1915	02/04/1915
Miscellaneous	No.4 Field Ambulance	02/04/1915	02/04/1915
Miscellaneous	No.4 Field Ambulance Evacuation Return 3pm	02/04/1915	02/04/1915
War Diary	Bethune	03/04/1915	03/04/1915
Miscellaneous	No.4 Field Ambulance	03/04/1915	03/04/1915
Miscellaneous	No.4 Field Ambulance Evacuation Return 3pm	03/04/1915	03/04/1915
War Diary	Bethune	04/04/1915	04/04/1915
Miscellaneous	No.4 Field Ambulance	04/04/1915	04/04/1915
Miscellaneous	No.4 Field Ambulance Evacuation Return 3pm	04/04/1915	04/04/1915
War Diary	Bethune	05/04/1915	05/04/1915
Miscellaneous	No.4 Field Ambulance	05/04/1915	05/04/1915
Miscellaneous	No.4 Field Ambulance Evacuation Return 3pm	05/04/1915	05/04/1915
War Diary	Bethune	06/04/1915	06/04/1915
Miscellaneous	No.4 Field Ambulance	06/04/1915	06/04/1915
Miscellaneous	No.4 Field Ambulance Evacuation Return 3pm	06/04/1915	06/04/1915
War Diary	Bethune	07/04/1915	07/04/1915
Miscellaneous	No.4 Field Ambulance	07/04/1915	07/04/1915
Miscellaneous	No.4 Field Ambulance Evacuation Return 3pm	07/04/1915	07/04/1915
War Diary	Bethune	08/04/1915	08/04/1915
Miscellaneous	No.4 Field Ambulance	08/04/1915	08/04/1915
Miscellaneous	No.4 Field Ambulance Evacuation Return 3pm	08/04/1915	08/04/1915
War Diary	Bethune	09/04/1915	09/04/1915
Miscellaneous	No.4 Field Ambulance	09/04/1915	09/04/1915
Miscellaneous	No.4 Field Ambulance Evacuation Return 3pm	09/04/1915	09/04/1915
War Diary	Bethune	10/04/1915	10/04/1915
Miscellaneous	No.4 Field Ambulance	10/04/1915	10/04/1915
Miscellaneous	No.4 Field Ambulance Evacuation Return 3pm	10/04/1915	10/04/1915
Miscellaneous	No.4 Field Ambulance	10/04/1915	10/04/1915
War Diary	Bethune	11/04/1915	11/04/1915
Miscellaneous	No.4 Field Ambulance	11/04/1915	11/04/1915
Miscellaneous	No.4 Field Ambulance Evacuation Return	11/04/1915	11/04/1915
Miscellaneous	No.4 Field Ambulance Evacuation Return 3pm	11/04/1915	11/04/1915
War Diary	Bethune	12/04/1915	12/04/1915
Miscellaneous	No.4 Field Ambulance	12/04/1915	12/04/1915
Miscellaneous	No.4 Field Ambulance Evacuation Return 3pm	12/04/1915	12/04/1915
War Diary	Bethune	13/04/1915	13/04/1915
Miscellaneous	No.4 Field Ambulance	13/04/1915	13/04/1915
Miscellaneous	No.4 Field Ambulance Evacuation Return 3pm	13/04/1915	13/04/1915
War Diary	Bethune	14/04/1915	14/04/1915
Miscellaneous	No.4 Field Ambulance Evacuation Return 3pm	14/04/1915	14/04/1915
War Diary	Bethune	15/04/1915	15/04/1915
Miscellaneous	No.4 Field Ambulance	15/04/1915	15/04/1915
Miscellaneous	No.4 Field Ambulance Evacuation Return 3pm	15/04/1915	15/04/1915
War Diary	Bethune	16/04/1915	16/04/1915
Miscellaneous	No.4 Field Ambulance Evacuation Return 3pm	16/04/1915	16/04/1915
Miscellaneous	No.4 Field Ambulance	16/04/1915	16/04/1915

War Diary	Bethune	17/04/1915	17/04/1915
Miscellaneous	No.4 Field Ambulance	17/04/1915	17/04/1915
Miscellaneous	No.4 Field Ambulance Evacuation Return 3pm	17/04/1915	17/04/1915
Miscellaneous	Bethune	18/04/1915	18/04/1915
War Diary	No.4 Field Ambulance	18/04/1915	18/04/1915
Miscellaneous	No.4 Field Ambulance Evacuation Return 3pm	18/04/1915	18/04/1915
War Diary	Bethune	19/04/1915	19/04/1915
Miscellaneous	No.4 Field Ambulance Evacuation Return 3pm	19/04/1915	19/04/1915
Miscellaneous	No.4 Field Ambulance	19/04/1915	19/04/1915
War Diary	Bethune	20/04/1915	20/04/1915
Miscellaneous	No.4 Field Ambulance	20/04/1915	20/04/1915
Miscellaneous	No.4 Field Ambulance Evacuation Return 9am	20/04/1915	20/04/1915
War Diary	Bethune	21/04/1915	21/04/1915
War Diary	Bethune	22/04/1915	22/04/1915
Miscellaneous	No.4 Field Ambulance	21/04/1915	21/04/1915
Miscellaneous	No.4 Field Ambulance Evacuation Return 3pm	21/04/1915	21/04/1915
War Diary	Bethune	22/04/1915	22/04/1915
Miscellaneous	No.4 Field Ambulance	22/04/1915	22/04/1915
Miscellaneous	No.4 Field Ambulance Evacuation Return 9.am	22/04/1915	22/04/1915
Miscellaneous	No.4 Field Ambulance Evacuation Return 3pm	22/04/1915	22/04/1915
War Diary	Bethune	23/04/1915	23/04/1915
Miscellaneous	No.4 Field Ambulance	23/04/1915	23/04/1915
Miscellaneous	No.4 Field Ambulance Evacuation Return 3pm	23/04/1915	23/04/1915
War Diary	Bethune	24/04/1915	24/04/1915
Miscellaneous	No.4 Field Ambulance	24/04/1915	24/04/1915
Miscellaneous	No.4 Field Ambulance Evacuation Return 3pm	24/04/1915	24/04/1915
Miscellaneous	Bethune	25/04/1915	25/04/1915
Miscellaneous	No.4 Field Ambulance	25/04/1915	25/04/1915
Miscellaneous	No.4 Field Ambulance Evacuation Return 9am	25/04/1915	25/04/1915
Miscellaneous	No.4 Field Ambulance Evacuation Return 3pm	25/04/1915	25/04/1915
Miscellaneous	Bethune	26/04/1915	26/04/1915
Miscellaneous	No.4 Field Ambulance	26/04/1915	26/04/1915
Miscellaneous	No.4 Field Ambulance Evacuation Return	26/04/1915	26/04/1915
Miscellaneous	No.4 Field Ambulance Evacuation Return 3pm	26/04/1915	26/04/1915
War Diary	Bethune	26/04/1915	27/04/1915
Miscellaneous	No.4 Field Ambulance	27/04/1915	27/04/1915
Miscellaneous	No.4 Field Ambulance Evacuation Return 9am	27/04/1915	27/04/1915
Miscellaneous	No.4 Field Ambulance Evacuation Return 3pm	27/04/1915	27/04/1915
War Diary	Bethune	28/04/1915	28/04/1915
Miscellaneous	No.4 Field Ambulance	28/04/1915	28/04/1915
Miscellaneous	No.4 Field Ambulance Evacuation Return 9am	28/04/1915	28/04/1915
Miscellaneous	No.4 Field Ambulance Evacuation Return 3pm	28/04/1915	28/04/1915
War Diary	Bethune	29/04/1915	29/04/1915
Miscellaneous	No.4 Field Ambulance	29/04/1915	29/04/1915
Miscellaneous	No.4 Field Ambulance Evacuation Return	29/04/1915	29/04/1915
Miscellaneous	No.4 Field Ambulance Evacuation Return 3pm	29/04/1915	29/04/1915
War Diary	Bethune	30/04/1915	30/04/1915
Miscellaneous	No.4 Field Ambulance	30/04/1915	30/04/1915
Miscellaneous	No.4 Field Ambulance Evacuation Return	30/04/1915	30/04/1915
Miscellaneous	No.4 Field Ambulance Evacuation Return 3pm	30/04/1915	30/04/1915
Miscellaneous	List Of Operations Performed		
Miscellaneous	April 1st-30th Operations		

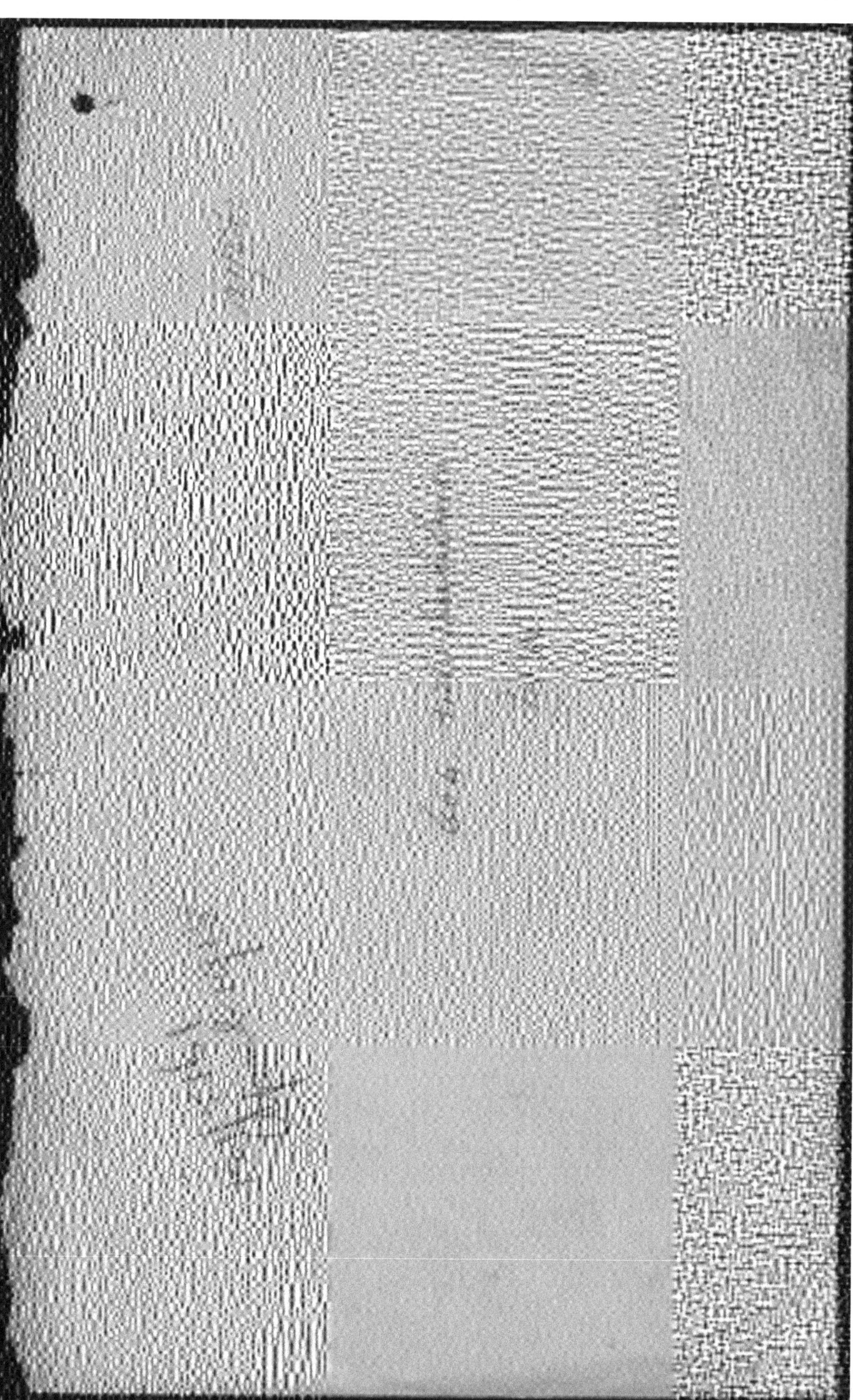

Army Form C. 2118.

WAR DIARY
or
INTELLIGENCE SUMMARY.
(Erase heading not required.)

Instructions regarding War Diaries and Intelligence Summaries are contained in F.S. Regs., Part II. and the Staff Manual respectively. Title pages will be prepared in manuscript.

Hour, Date, Place	Summary of Events and Information	Remarks and references to Appendices
April 1st, 1915 BETHUNE	No of casualties 39. Major W. R. Wilson 4th R.W.F. Capt. F.M Greenhill, 1st L.N. Lancs. } Evacuated by No 7. Revd. Sir R.J.M. Meyler, 2nd Welsh Regs. } M.A.C. 2nd Lt. A.H Macgregor, 1st London Scottish. Major J.M Young, (D.A.D.M.G, 1st Div) returned to duty.	

No 4 Field Ambulance

Evacuation Return 3 pm

Officers 4
Other Ranks Lying 5
Sitting 4

06 Nov Motor Convoy
1-4-15

Capt R A M C
O.C. No 4 Field Amb

Army Form C. 2118.

WAR DIARY
or
INTELLIGENCE SUMMARY.
(Erase heading not required.)

Instructions regarding War Diaries and Intelligence Summaries are contained in F.S. Regs., Part II and the Staff Manual respectively. Title pages will be prepared in manuscript.

Hour, Date, Place	Summary of Events and Information	Remarks and references to Appendices
April 2nd 1915. BETHUNE	Capt. J.J. O'Keeffe, R.A.M.C. proceeded to Advanced Dressing Station, to take charge of Beuvry Sub-Division in neut of Capt. W.H. Boyce R.A.M.C. who returned to Headquarters in accordance with instructions received from A.D.M.S. 2nd Div. The following is a copy of the order issued to Capt. W.H. Boyce R.A.M.C. — "The following measures have been received from A.D.M.S. 2nd Div. 'Until autumnus medical from field for Army Capt. W.H. Boyce R.A.M.C. will proceed to England forthwith, reporting himself at War Office on arrival.' Date of departure to be upon this office". Capt J.J. O'Keeffe R.A.M.C. is being sent there in charge of Beuvry Sub-Division, and no long relying by him, you are report to this office. No & 70 Ambulance	

WAR DIARY
or
INTELLIGENCE SUMMARY.
(Erase heading not required.)

Army Form C. 2118.

Hour, Date, Place	Summary of Events and Information	Remarks and references to Appendices
April 2nd, 1915. BETHUNE. (Continued)	Lieut. N.N.P. Matom, RAMC returned to duty from leave. Admd 2nd Div and G.O.C. 2nd Div visited officers' Dressing Station, accompanied by Maton-in-Chief Rt Rev. The Lord Bishop of London paid a private visit to the Officers' Dressing Station accompanied by Rev. P.M. Waggett. No. 052803 Sgt. G. Steward, A.S.C. (M.T.) arrived for duty. No. of casualties 15. Capt. C.M.H. Madery for Coldm. Gds. (Gun L. Leg) Lieut. A.N. Smith, R.A.M.C. (Shell lives legs) 2nd Lt. S. Craven 1st London (Three air cmds) Lieut W.G. Higgins, A.S.C. Returned to duty 2nd Lt. M.j. Cox, 1st R. Berks.	Evacuated by No. 7 M.A.C.

WAR DIARY
or
INTELLIGENCE SUMMARY

(Erase heading not required)

Summary of Events and Information

No. 4 Field Ambulance

No. of sick and wounded admitted, by Units, during 24 hours ended 9am. 2/4/15.

Unit - 2nd Divn.	Officers Sick	Officers Wnd	Other Rks. Sick	Other Rks. Wnd	Remarks
2nd Grenadier Guards	-	-	-	1	Officers to duty
2nd Coldstream Guards	-	-	1	1	D.A.D.M.S. 1st D.V.
3rd Coldstream Guards	-	-	1	2	(Major J. M. YOUNG)
1st Herts	-	-	-	1	Other Ranks
2nd S. Staffs	-	-	1	-	to duty:
4th Kings	-	-	1	-	to light duty
R.F.A. 56th Batty	-	-	1	-	1 5th Kings
A.C.C. 2nd Divn	-	-	2	-	1 1st K.R.R.
					1 1st R. Berks
					4 8th City of Lond.
Totals	-	-	7	5	
Other Divisions					
1st Coldstream Guards	-	1	-	-	
London Scottish	-	1	-	-	
1st Black Watch	1	-	-	-	
7th City of London	-	-	1	1	
8th City of London	-	-	-	1	
R.E.(T.) 4th Lond 70 Co.	-	1	-	-	
R.A.M.C. att. 4 Seaforths	1	-	-	-	
Totals	2	3	1	2	

Prevailing Disease - Nil
No. with foot troubles - Nil

	Sick	Wnd
Admitted Officers	2	3
Other Rks.	8	7
Evac'd Officers	4	1
Other Rks.	14	8
Remaining Officers	20	4
Other Rks.	37	17

Evac'd by M.A.C.:-
  Officers - 4
  Other Rks - 15
Retd to Duty:-
  Officers - 1
  Other Rks - 1
Retd Light duty:-
  Other Rks - 7

2nd Lt. A. H. MACGREGOR, 1st London Scottish, G.S.W. Thighs
" " A. GRAY, 1st Black Watch, Inflam. of Pharynx
Lieut. W. S. GARDEN, R.A.M.C. att. 4 Seaforths, Concussion
Major H. H. S. MARSH, R.E.(T.) 4 Lond. 70 Co, Shell wnd Rt Hand & Abdomen
Capt. C. M. H. MASSEY, 1st Colds. Gds. G.S.W. L. Legg

P.H. Lloyd Jones
Capt. R.A.M.C.
O.C. No. 4 Fd Ambce

A.D.M.S. 2nd Divn
2/4/15.

No 4 Field Ambulance

Evacuation Return 3pm

Officers 3 *

Other Ranks Lying 10
           Sitting 4

Includes 1 Officer for evacuation from the Main Dressing Station.

O.C. Noy Motor Convoy
2-4-15

P. H. Lloyd Jones
Capt. R.A.M.C.
O.C. No 4 Field Amb.

Army Form C. 2118.

WAR DIARY
or
INTELLIGENCE SUMMARY.
(Erase heading not required.)

Instructions regarding War Diaries and Intelligence Summaries are contained in F.S. Regs., Part II and the Staff Manual respectively. Title pages will be prepared in manuscript.

Hour, Date, Place	Summary of Events and Information	Remarks and references to Appendices
3rd April, 1915. BETHUNE.	Number of casualties – 33. Lieut. T. A. de V. Robertson 55th Rifles. Capt. G.S. Bull 55th Rifles ⎫ Capt. S/S. R. Michelsen 114th Batty., R.G.A. ⎬ Returned to duty. Major R.A.M. Hall, 7th Mtn. Batty, R.G.A. ⎪ Capt. H.S. Cormack, I.M.S. ⎭ Lieut. H. Marion-Crawford, 101 Field Coy. No. 26303 Driver Goose, C.T., A.S.C. ⎫ Proceeded to No.1 No. 26235 " Ruwed, P. A.S.C. ⎬ Reserve Park for duty. No. 31302 L/Cpl. Sefton, B. A.M.C. ⎫ Proceeded to Advanced " T/25676 Dr. Ullich H. " ⎪ Horse Transport " 325 " Clarke, M. " ⎬ Depôt for duty. " 18267 " Hargreaves T. " ⎪ " T/23558 " Hockins S. " ⎪ " 30160 " Renville H. " ⎭	

Army Form C. 2118.

WAR DIARY
or
INTELLIGENCE SUMMARY.

(Erase heading not required.)

Hour, Date, Place	Summary of Events and Information	Remarks and references to Appendices
April 3rd 1915 BETHUNE. (Continued)	Capt. M. W. Boyce, R.A.M.C. proceeded to England for duty, under instructions from A.D.M.S. 2nd Divn No. 789 d/=/4/15	

No. 4 Field Ambulance

No. of sick and wounded, by Units, admitted to No 4 Field Ambulance during 24 hours ended 9 a.m. 3/4/15.

Unit - 2nd Division	Officers Sick	Officers Wounded	Other Rks. Sick	Other Rks. Wounded	Remarks.
2nd Grenadier Guards.	-	-	-	1	Officers to Duty:-
2nd Coldstream Guards	-	-	3	-	1. A.S.C. (Lahore Div).
3rd Coldstream "	-	-	1	-	1. 1st R. Berks.
1st Irish Guards.	-	-	2	-	Other Rks. to Duty.
1st Herts.	-	-	3	-	1. 6th City of London.
5th Kings	-	-	2	-	To Light Duty:-
2nd S. Staffs	-	-	2	-	1. 2nd Gren. Gds.
R.G.A. 35th Hy. Batt.	-	-	1	-	3. 1st Herts.
R.E. 11th Fd. Co.	-	-	-	1	1. 7th Kings
A.S.C. (H.Q.)	-	-	1	-	
" 35th Coy.	-	-	3	-	
A.C.C.	-	-	1	-	
Total.	-	-	19	2	
2nd Division					
8th City of London	-	-	-	1	
6th " " "	-	-	5	5	
7th London	1	-	-	-	
1st Coldstream Gds.	1	-	-	-	
1st Queens	-	-	1	-	
R.F.A. 17th Batt.	1	-	-	-	
Total.	3	-	6	6	

Prevailing Disease - Nil
No. with foot troubles - Nil.

Evac'd by M.A.C.:-
  Officers. 3
  Other Rks. 15
Ret'd duty:-
  Officers 2
  Other Rks. 1
Ret'd Light Duty
  Other Rks. 5

	Sick	Wound.
Admitted Officers	3	-
" Other Rks.	25	8
Evac'd Officers	3	3
" Other Rks.	15	6
Remng. Officers	20	1
" Other Rks.	47	19

Capt. R.B.T. CRAWFORD, 1st Colds. Gds.   Sprained Ankle.
    " H.G. HEAD, 7th London Regt.   " Thigh.
2nd Lt. K. THORBURN, 17th Batty R.F.A.   Influenza.

A.D.M.S. 2nd Divn.
3/4/15.

P.H. Lloyd Jones.
Capt. R.A.M.C.
O.C. No. 4 Fd. Amb.

No 4 Field Ambulance

Evacuation Return 3pm

Other Ranks Lying 5
           Sitting 8.

O.C. No 7 Motor Convoy } 3
  3-4-15

for Lieut
    Capt RAMC
    O.C. No 4 Field Amb

Army Form C. 2118.

WAR DIARY
or
INTELLIGENCE SUMMARY.
(Erase heading not required.)

Instructions regarding War Diaries and Intelligence Summaries are contained in F. S. Regs., Part II. and the Staff Manual respectively. Title pages will be prepared in manuscript.

Hour, Date, Place	Summary of Events and Information	Remarks and references to Appendices
4th April, 1915. BETHUNE.	No of Casualties = 27. 2nd Lieut. J. Muirhead for BC Match (Skull and Face) Evacuated by No 7 M.A.C. Lieut H.D. Willis R.A.M.C. " W.S. Gardner R.A.M.C. 2nd Lt N. Cullwick, 470th Batt. R.F.A. } Returned to duty Capt. R.J.B. Crawford 101 Cordon Gds. Lieut F.A. Clifford 11th 70 Co. R.E. Lieut N.H.P. Morton R.A.M.C. proceeded to 11th Bde. R.F.A. for temporary duty.	

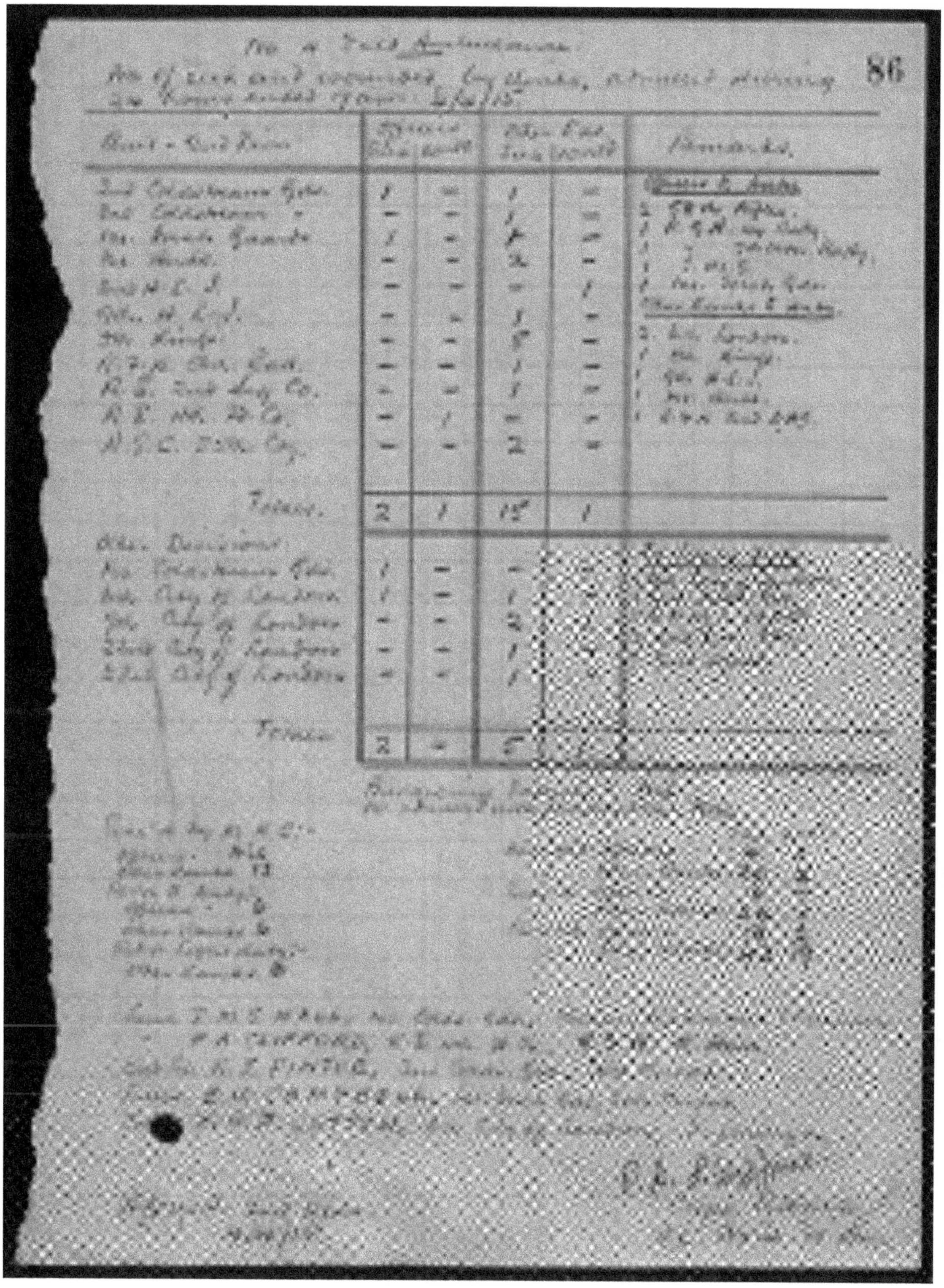

86

No 4 Field Ambulance.

Evacuation Return 3pm.

Other Ranks Lying 4
            Sitting 6.

1 Officers car may be required, will notify later.

O.C. No 4 Motor Convoy.
3pm 4-4-15

J S Murray
Capt RAMC
p O.C. No 4 Fd Ambl

Army Form C. 2118.

WAR DIARY
or
INTELLIGENCE SUMMARY.
(Erase heading not required.)

Instructions regarding War Diaries and Intelligence Summaries are contained in F.S. Regs., Part II. and the Staff Manual respectively. Title pages will be prepared in manuscript.

Hour, Date, Place	Summary of Events and Information	Remarks and references to Appendices
5th April, 1915. BETHUNE	Casualties – 18. Capt. E.C. Ball, 7th City of London (Fractures) 2nd Lt. N.M. Rushworth, 7th City of London (G.S.W. arm) } Evac'd by No. 7 M.A.C. Lieut. R.N. Brien, 4th R.W.F. (Neurasthenia) Capt. Lord A.R. de Trafford, 1st S.W.B. Lieut. E.W. Ashby, 6th City of London " H. Gray, 1st Black Watch " Bird Hall, 1st Coldm. Gds. } Returned to duty. Lieut. H.M. Cockcroft, R.A.M.C., arrived for duty. Rev. N.J. Fleming, S.C.F. (att. No.4 Fd Amb.) admitted to Officers' Dressing Station suffering from Bronchitis Catarrhus	

No. 4 Field Ambulance.
Return of sick and wounded admitted, by Units, during 24 hours ended 9 am, 5/4/15

Unit. 2nd Divn	Officers Sick	Officers Wnd	Other Ranks Sick	Other Ranks Wnd	Remarks
2nd Coldstream Gds	-	-	-	1	Officers to Duty
3rd Coldstream "	-	-	1	-	1 2nd Colds. Gds.
1st Irish Guards	-	-	1	1	1 R.E. 11th Fd. Co.
2nd S. Staffs	-	-	1	2	2 RAMC
R.F.A 15th Batt.	-	-	1	-	1 R.F.A. 15th Batt.
5th Batt.	-	-	1	-	Other Rks to duty
R.G.A. 35th Hy Batt	-	-	1	-	1 R.G.A. 35 Co
A.S.C. (M.T.)	-	-	2	-	
3.E Lancs att 2nd S/Staff	-	1	-	-	
Total	-	1	7	4	

Other Divs					To light duty
1st Bl. Watch	-	1	-	-	6 6th. City of London.
7th City of London	-	-	1	-	1 3rd Colds Gds.
6th " "	-	-	1	-	1 ASC
5th " "	-	-	1	-	1 7th London.
4th R.W.F. w.y	1	-	-	-	1 1st Herts.
Total	1	2	3	-	1 2nd S. Staffs.

Previously Remaining Nos.
No. accn foot trouches - 1
	Sick	Wnd
Admitted Officers	1	3
Other Rks	10	4
Evac'd Officers	4	2
Other Rks	17	3
Remng Officers	15	3
Other Rks	34	16

Evac'd by M.A.C.
Officers 1
Other Rks 11
Rtnd to Duty
Officers 5
Other Rks 18
Rtnd to Lt duty
Other Rks 10

2nd L. T. MUIRHEAD 1st Bl. Watch. Sick Wnd Face.
" " H. R. C. MARTIN 3 E. Lancs att Ams. S. Staffs. G.S.W. Fav.
" " T. C. W. MINSHALL, 4th R.W.F. Influenza.
" " H. M. RUSHWORTH, 7th City of London. G.S.W. R. Arm.

J S Munson
Capt. RAMC
For OC No. 4 Fd Amb

A.D.M.S. 2nd Divn
5/4/15.

New Field Ambulance

Evacuation Return 3 pm.

Officers 3

Other Ranks Lying 4
           Sitting 3.

O.C. 16/y Motor Convoy } 3
5-4-15   } 3
                        } 3

Don Pth...ple
Lt ~~Capt~~ A Webb
for O.C. New Field Amb

Army Form C. 2118.

WAR DIARY
or
INTELLIGENCE SUMMARY.
(Erase heading not required.)

Instructions regarding War Diaries and Intelligence Summaries are contained in F. S. Regs., Part II. and the Staff Manual respectively. Title pages will be prepared in manuscript.

Hour, Date, Place	Summary of Events and Information	Remarks and references to Appendices
6th April 1916 BETHUNE	Number of casualties - 30. Capt. T. Donnelly, Lahore Divl Am. Col. Neuralgia) Evac'd 2nd Lt. H.R.E. Martin, 3rd E. Lancs att. 2 S. Staffs Sn:7 M.A.C. Major Z.C. Pope, D.S.O., 114th Batty R.G.A. Capt. H.E. Head, 7th London Regt. } Returned to duty. 2nd Lt. K. Thorburn, 17th Batty R.F.A.	

No 4 Field Ambulance.

Nr. of Sick and wounded admitted, by Units, during 24 hours ended 9am. 6/4/15.

Units and R.̲	Officers Sick	Wnd.	Other Rks Sick	Wnd.	Remarks.
2nd Coldstream Gds	–	–	2	–	Officers to duty.
3rd Coldstream Gds	–	–	1	–	1 1st S.W.B
1st Irish Gds.	–	–	–	2	1 6th C. of London.
1st Herts.	–	–	5	–	1 1st R. Welch.
1st K.R.R.	–	–	2	–	1 1st Colds. Gds.
2nd R. Inniskg. Fus.	1	–	–	–	Other Rks. to duty.
5th Kings	–	–	4	–	1 1st Irish Gds.
7th Kings.	–	–	1	1	1 3rd Colds.
R.F.A 44 Bde.	–	–	2	–	1 ACC.
R.E. 170th Coy.	–	–	1	–	To Light duty.
A.S.C. 111th Coy	–	–	1	–	1 6th Kings.
R.E. 2nd Sig Coy	–	–	1	–	1 R.E. 2 Sig Co.
R.A.M.C. (San Sec)	–	–	1	–	1 1st Kings
S.C.F. (No4 F.A)	1	–	–	–	1 5th Kings
					1 2nd S. Staffs.
					1 ACC.
					1 R.G.A. 35 Hy Batt.
Totals	2	–	21	3	

Other Divs.
4th R.W. Fus.	1	–	–	–
5th City of London	–	–	1	–
6th " " "	–	–	1	–
R.G.A Lahore D.A.C.	1	–	–	–
Total.	2	–	2	–

Evac'd by D.H.Q.
 Officers 3
 Other Rks 8
To Duty:
 Officers 4
 Other Rks 5
To light duty
 Other Rks 8

Prevailing Disease: Nil
No with foot troubles: Nil

	Sick	Wnd.
Admitted Officers	4	–
Other Rks	23	3
Evac'd Officers	6	1
Other Rks	14	8
Remaining Officers	13	2
Other Rks	45	11

Lieut R.H. OWEN, 4th R.W.F. Neurasthenia
C.H. DANIELS, 2nd R Inniskg. Fus. N.Y.D Pyrexia.
Capt. T. DONNELLY, Lahore Div. A.C. R.G.A. Neuralgia
Revd. H.T. FLEMING, S.C.F. a/c No 4 F. Amb. Bron Catarrhal

A.D.M.S. 2nd Divn
6/4/15

Capt. R.A.M.C
O.C. No 4 Fd. Amb.

No 4 Field Ambulance

Evacuation Return 3 pm

Officers. 2.
Other Ranks Lying 1
Sitting 3.

O.C. No 4 Motor Convoy
6-4-15

for Capt R.A.M.C.
O.C. No 4 Field Ambulance

Army Form C. 2118.

WAR DIARY
or
INTELLIGENCE SUMMARY.
(Erase heading not required.)

Instructions regarding War Diaries and Intelligence Summaries are contained in F.S. Regs, Part II and the Staff Manual respectively. Title pages will be prepared in manuscript.

Hour, Date, Place	Summary of Events and Information	Remarks and references to Appendices
7th April, 1915. BETHUNE.	No of casualties — 23. Lieut E. D. McKenzie, 1st Scots Gds. (measles) Major M Stewart, 1st Camerons, (Shell wound Shrapnel) Sent to 2nd Lt. T. C. N. Minichiello, 4 R. M. 7 (Influenza) by No. 7 M.A.C Lieut L R Hargraves 1st Irish Gds. returned to duty. 4 Officers and 20 men R.A.M.C. (T.) of the 1/2 London Div arrived for purpose of instruction and observation of the working of a Field Ambulance. The transport which brought this party took back the party which was sent for similar reason on the 2nd instant.	

No. 4 Field Ambulance.

No. of sick and wounded admitted during 24 hours
9 a.m. 7/4/15

Unit: 2nd Divn	Officers Sick	Officers Wnd	Other Rks Sick	Other Rks Wnd	Remarks
1st Herts	–	–	5	–	Officers to duty.
1st K.R.R.	–	–	2	–	R.G.A. 114 Batt.
9th H.L.I.	–	–	1	–	7th London Regt.
2nd Oxfords	–	–	–	1	R.F.A. 17th Batt.
R.F.A. 34th Bde.	–	–	3	–	Other Rks Duty.
A.C.C.	–	–	1	–	R.G.A. 35th Hy Batt.
RAMC (5th Fd Am)	–	–	1	–	5th Kings.
1st R. Berks.	1	–	–	–	1st Herts.
Total	1	–	13	1	
Other Divisions.					To Light duty.
10th Hussars att. } A.S.C. 1 Div Train }	1	–	–	–	1 23rd London.
6th City of London	–	–	3	–	1 6th London
8th City of London	–	–	2	–	2 5th Kings.
6th London	1	1	–	–	1 R.E. 2 Sig Co.
1st Cameron.	–	–	–	–	
Total	2	1	5	–	

Prevailing Disease. Nil.
No. with foot troubles – 4.

Evac'd by M.A.C.
  Officers – 2
  Other Ras. 4
Ret'd to duty
  Officers 3
  Other Rks. 3
Ret'd light duty.
  Other Rks. 4

	Sick	Wnd
Admitted Officers	3	1
Other Rks.	18	1
Evac'd Officers	4	1
Other Rks	11	1
Remng. Officers	12	2
Other Rks.	52	11

Capt. C.R. MOLYNEUX, 10th Hussars att. A.S.C. 1st Div Trn. Dysentery.
2nd Lt. F.H. DICKINSON, 6th London, Synovitis L. Knee.
  " " H.D. STEED, 1st R. Berks. Caries Dentis.
Major W.M. STEWART, (1st Camerons (Staff Capt.) Shell wnd R. Shdr.
  (Ferozepore Brigade)

ADMS 2nd Divn
7/4/15.

P.A. Hodgson
Capt. RAMC
O.C. No. 4 Fd. Ambce

No 14 Field Ambulance.

Evacuation Return 3pm.

Officers :- 2.

Other Ranks: Lying. 7.
           Sitting. 5.

O.C. No 4 Motor Convoy }
3pm. 7-4-15   }

W W Cockcroft
Lieut
Lieut R.A.M.C.
for O.C. No 14 Field Amb

Army Form C. 2118.

WAR DIARY
or
INTELLIGENCE SUMMARY.
(Erase heading not required.)

Instructions regarding War Diaries and Intelligence Summaries are contained in F.S. Regs., Part II. and the Staff Manual respectively. Title pages will be prepared in manuscript.

Hour, Date, Place	Summary of Events and Information	Remarks and references to Appendices
5th April, 1915. BETHUNE.	Number of Casualties - 20. 2nd Lieut N.M. Caffyn, 4th E. Surrey (Denmark) Evac'd " " A.C.M. Innes 1st Irish Gds. (Neurasthenia) by No.7 m.A.C 2nd Lt E.E. Redding 7th Kings Lieut. E.M. Campbell 1st Irish Gds. } Returned to duty. 2nd Lt R.J. Pinto 2nd Cold Gds. 2nd Lt N.B. Steed, 1st R. Berks. Major R.E.S. Prentice 2nd N.F.S. Brigade major 2nd Brigade admitted Officers Divisional Station with Shell wound Arm.	

No 4 Field Ambulance.   50

No. of sick and wounded admitted, by Units, during
24 hours ended 9 am. 8/4/15.

Units - 2nd Div.	Officers Sick/Wnd		Other Ranks Sick/Wnd		Remarks
2nd Grenadier Gds.	–	–	3	1	Officers to Duty
2nd Coldstream Gds.	–	–	1	–	1 1st Grndr. Gds.
3rd Coldstream Gds.	–	–	1	–	Other Ranks Duty
1st Irish Gds.	1	–	1	–	1 R.E. 2 Sig. Co.
1st H.L.I.	–	–	–	1	1 Rif. Bde.
2nd S. Staffs.	–	–	1	–	1 A.S.C. } 4 TT
M.M.G. Sec. No 1 Bat.	–	–	1	–	1 5th Kings.
R.G.A. 7th Mtn Bat.	–	–	1	–	1 ACC
Total	1	–	10	2	
Other Divisions					To Light Duty
1st Scots Gds.	1	–	–	–	1 R.F.A. 50th Batty.
2nd Black Watch.	1	–	–	–	1 7th London.
6th City of London.	–	–	1	–	2 5th Kings.
8th do	–	–	1	–	1 13th Hrs.
22nd London.	1	–	–	–	1 6th City of London.
4 East Surrey (att)	1	–	–	–	
1 R.H. Lancs	–	–	–	–	
R.F.A. 47th Bde.	–	–	1	–	
Total	4	–	3	–	

Prevailing Disease Nil
No. admitted with frost bite/trenches Nil

Tdec'd M.A.C.
  Officers – 3 × 1 in Special car = 4
  Other Ranks. 10.
Ret'd to duty
  Officers 1.
  Other Ranks 5.
Ret'd Light duty:
  Other Ranks 6.

Admitted Officers   5
           Other Ranks 13   2
Tdec'd   Officers   3
          Other Ranks 19   2
Remaining Officers   14   –
          Other Ranks 16 11

Lieut. E.D. MCKENZIE, 1st Scots. Gds.   Measles.
2nd Lt. A.C.W. INNES, 1st Irish Gds.   Rheumatism
  "   T.C. CAMPBELL 2nd Bl. Watch.   Rheumatic fever.
  "   A.M. COFFYN, 4 E. Surrey att.   16 G. House. N.Y.D. Skin
Lt. Col. E.J. PREVITE, 22 London.   Company Sig. al. Crown

A.D.M.S. 2nd Divn.   P.A. Lloyd Jones
  8/4/15.   Capt. R.A.M.C.
                                           A.C. T.O. 4 Fd. Amb.

No 4 Field Ambulance
  "

Evacuation Return 3pm.
  "

Officers : 2

Other Ranks Lying   3
         Sitting. 6

O.C. No 4 Motor Convoy
8-4-15

Bon McAnee
   Lieut
for Capt R.A.M.C.
O.C. No 4 Field Amb

Army Form C. 2118.

WAR DIARY
or
INTELLIGENCE SUMMARY.
(Erase heading not required.)

Instructions regarding War Diaries and Intelligence Summaries are contained in F.S. Regs., Part II and the Staff Manual respectively. Title pages will be prepared in manuscript.

Hour, Date, Place	Summary of Events and Information	Remarks and references to Appendices
9th April, 1915. BETHUNE	Number of Casualties – 16. Major R.E.S. Prentice, 2nd. N.S.I. (Brigade Major 2nd Bde) (Shell wound Arm) 2nd Lt J S Cameron, 1st L N Lancs (Mesopotamia) Evacuated by tr. to 7 M.A.C. No. 9045 Pte A. Long, R.A.M.C (4th. Field Amb.ce) Evacuated by tr. 7 M.A.C. to Base with Hernia.	[signature]

No. 4 Field Ambulance.
No. of sick and wounded admitted, by Units, during 24 hours ended 9 am. 9/4/15.

	Officers Sick	Officers Wnd.	Other Rks. Sick	Other Rks. Wnd.	Remarks
1st. Irish Guards	—	—	2	—	Officers to Duty.
2nd Colds. Guards	—	—	1	—	1 7th. Kings
3rd Colds. Guards	—	—	—	1	1 2nd Colds. Gds.
1st. Herts.	—	—	—	1	1 1st. Irish Gds.
2nd Oxfords.	1	—	—	—	1 1st. R. Berks.
2nd Worces.	1	—	—	—	Other Rks to Light Duty.
2nd H.L.I.	—	1	—	—	1 R.F.A. 44th. Bde.
5th. Kings	—	—	1	—	1 A.S.C. (M.T.)
R.F.A. 2 D.A.C.	—	—	2	—	1 A.S.C. 11th. Co.
RAMC (No. 47 FA)	—	—	1	—	1 2 Colds. Gds.
					1 5th Kings
					1 K.R.R.
Totals	2	1	7	2	
Other Divs.					Other Rks. to Duty.
15th County London	—	—	—	2	1 5th. Kings
5th. Royal Sussex.	—	1	—	—	1 Cty. London.
R.F.A. 5th Batt.	—	—	1	—	1 A.C.C.
					1 1st. Herts.
Totals	—	1	1	2	

Prevailing Disease. Nil
No. admitted with foot troubles. Nil

Evac'd by M.A.C.
 Officers 2
 Other Rks. 9
Ret'd to duty
 Officers 4
 Other Rks. 4
Ret'd light duty.
 Other Rks. 6

	Sick	Wnd
Admitted Officers	2	2
Other Rks	8	2
Evacuated Officers	6	1
Other Rks	18	1
Remaining Officers	10	2
Other Rks	36	15

2nd Lt. W.J. EIGHTEEN, 2nd Oxfds. Myalgia
  "   " C. TYSON, 2nd Worcesters. Myalgia.
Major R.E.S. PRENTICE, 2nd H.L.I. (Bde. Maj. 2 Bde) Shell wnd Arm
Capt. T.B. HORNBLOWER, 5th R. Sussex, G.S.W. R. side of Thorax.

P.A. Lloyd Jones
Capt. RAMC.
O.C. No. 4 Fd. Amb.

ADMS, 2nd Divn
 9/4/15

No 4 Field Ambulance

Evacuation Return 3pm

Officers: 2

Other Ranks Lying: 8 4
                Sitting: 2

To No 4 Motor Convoy
9.4.15

Basil H Murphy
Lieut
for. O.C No 4 Field Ambl.

Army Form C. 2118.

WAR DIARY
or
INTELLIGENCE SUMMARY.
(Erase heading not required.)

Hour, Date, Place	Summary of Events and Information	Remarks and references to Appendices
18th April, 1915. BETHUNE.	Number of Casualties – 24. Capt. W.T. Knitic, 1st Black Watch (G.S.W. Back) Evacuated by No. 7 M.A.C. " B.T. Bathys, R.E. (G.S.W. R. Thigh) " T. Gifford, 2nd Black Watch (Colculi) Rev'd N.J. Fleming (S.C.F.) attached No. 4 to Ambu discharged from Hospital and proceeded on 7 days leave to England Capt. C.R. Molesena, 10th Hussars (Attached A.S.C. 1st Supt. Train) and – Capt. A.E.F. Lloyd, 1st R. Berks Returned to duty.	

No. 4 Field Ambulance
No. of sick and wounded, by Units, admitted during
24 hours ended 9 a.m. 10/4/15.

Unit - 2nd Divⁿ	Officers Sick	Officers Wnded	Other Rks. Sick	Other Rks. Wnded	Remarks
2nd Coldstream Gds.	—	—	1	—	Ret'd to duty.
3rd "	—	—	—	1	9th Bde R.F.A. - 1.
1st Irish Guards	—	—	2	—	M.M. & S. - 1.
1st Herts.	—	—	1	—	
5th Kings.	—	—	1	—	
9th N.L.I.	—	—	—	1	
2nd S. Staffs.	—	—	4	—	
1st R. Berks.	—	1	—	—	
R.G.A. 35th H. Batt.	—	—	2	—	
R.A.M.C. att. 9 Kings.	1	—	—	—	
" " 2 N.L.I.	1	—	—	—	
Total.	2	1	11	2	
Other Divisions					Ret'd light duty.
1st Black Watch.	—	1	—	—	6th London - 2.
2nd do	1	—	—	—	1st Herts - 4.
1st L.N. Lancs	1	—	—	—	70th B. R.F.A. - 1.
105 Mahratta L.I. att. }					8th London - 1.
129 Baluchis }	—	1	—	—	1st K.R.R. - 2.
6th City of London.	■	—	1	—	8th City Lnd. - 1
20th "	■	—	1	—	
4th London	1	—	—	—	
Corps of Interpreters att }	1	—	—	—	
XV Lancers }					
Total.	4	2	2	—	

Prevailing Disease - Nil
No. admitted with foot trouble - Nil.

Evac'd by M.A.C.
  Officers - 2
  Other Rks. 9
Ret'd duty:-
  Officers Nil
  Other Rks. 2
Ret'd light duty
  Other Ranks. 11.

	Sick	Wnd.
Admitted officers	6	3
" Other Rks.	13	2
Evac'd officers	1	1
" Other Rks.	19	3
Remaining officers	15	4
" Other Rks.	31	11.

A.D.M.S. 2nd Divⁿ
10/4/15.

P.T.O.

Capt. R.A.M.C.
O.C. No. 4 F^d Ambce

No 4 Field Ambulance.

Evacuation Return 3pm

Officers 3 (2 Lying / 1 Sitting)

Other Ranks Lying 5
Sitting 4

O.C. No 7 Motor Convoy
10.4.15

[signature]
Capt R.A.M.C
O.C. No 4 Field Ambl

No 4 Field Ambulance.

Officers admitted 10/4/15.
Major M.J. MAHONEY, RAMC. (att. 9th Kings), Pleurisy.
2nd Lt. J.S. CURWEN, 1st L.N. Lancs., Neurasthenia.
"   E.P.M. MOSLEY, 4th London, Dysentery.
Capt. W.T. KEDIE, 1st Black Watch, Wnd Back
"   T. GRIFFITHS, 2nd " " Calculi.
Lieut. A.C. JEPSON, RAMC (att 2 H.L.I.) Bron. Catarrhal.
2nd Lt. A.J. CONNOR, Corps of Interpreters } Asthma.
                    att XV Lancers

Capt. A.C.F. ISAAC, 1st R. Berks, Shell Wnd Hand.
"   A. DELINE, RADCLIFFE, 105 Mahratta L.I. } G.S.W. Chest.
                          att. 129 Baluchis.

P. A. Lloyd Jones.
Capt RAMC.
OC. No 4 Fd. Ambce

A.D.M.S. 2nd Divn
10/4/15. 9 am.

Army Form C. 2118.

WAR DIARY
or
INTELLIGENCE SUMMARY.
(Erase heading not required.)

Instructions regarding War Diaries and Intelligence Summaries are contained in F.S. Regs., Part II. and the Staff Manual respectively. Title pages will be prepared in manuscript.

Hour, Date, Place	Summary of Events and Information	Remarks and references to Appendices
11th April, 1915. BETHUNE.	G.O.C. 5th London Brigade inspected the Dressing Station. Casualties – 26. Major C.S. Lewis, A.S.C. 1st Scots Train (Rheumatic fever), 2nd Lt. W.E. Polchett, 1st Cameron (Piles) and 2nd Lt. E.R. Harris, 1st Kings (G.S.W. L. Leg) Evacuated by No. 7 M.A.C. Lieut C.H. Daniels, 2nd Lincoln Regt returned to duty. No 7638 Pte R. Pincott, R.A.M.C. proceeds to St. OMER for duty with No. 2 Ambulance Flotilla.	(RAD)

No. 4 Field Ambulance

Return of Sick & wounded, by Units, admitted during 24 hours ended 9.0 a.m. 11/4/15.

Units :- 2nd Div.	Officers		Other Ranks		Remarks
	Sick	Wded	Sick	Wded	
2 Coldstream Gds.	-	-	2	2	Rep. to duty :-
3rd " "	-	-	-	4	R.A.M.C. - 1
5th Kings	-	-	1	-	6th City of London - 1
2nd South Staffs.	-	-	4	-	1st Herts - 1
R.F.A. 70th Bty.	-	-	1	-	S.C.2 1st Field Amb. - 1
2nd Grenadier Gds.	-	-	-	2	10th Hussars attd.
1st Kings	1	1	-	-	A.S.C. 1st Div Train - 1
R.A.M.C. attd 1st F.A.	1	-	-	-	1st R. Berks - 1
R.E. (29th Coy)	1	-	-	-	
9th M.F.A.	-	-	-	1	
2nd Ox. Bucks.	-	-	-	1	
	3	1	8	10	

Other Divisions :-					
					Rep. to Light Duty :-
1st Cameron Hdrs.	1	-	-	-	7th HK Bty. R.F.A. - 1
17th County of London	-	-	-	1	1 Herts - 1
4th Seaforth Hldrs.	1	-	-	-	2 Gren. Gds - 2
A.S.C. 1st Div Train	1	-	-	-	2 Colds. Gds - 1
	3	-	-	1	

Prevailing disease - Nil
No. admitted with Foot troubles - Nil

	Sick	Wded
Admitted Officers	4	3
" Other Ranks	8	11
Evacd. Officers	3	3
" Other Ranks	17	4
Remaining Officers	16	4
" Other Ranks	22	18

Evacd. by M.A.C. :-
Officers - 3
Other Ranks - 13

Rep. to Duty :-
Officers - 3
Other Ranks - 3

Rep. to Light Duty :-
Other Ranks - 5

Officers admitted 11/4/15.
Capt. S. MARTIN R.A.M.C. attached 1st M.F.A. — Malaria.
" B.C. BATTYE, 2nt. S. 00 R.E. — S.S.W.R. Thigh
2nd. Lt. V.E. PATCHETT 1st Cameron Hdrs. — Dysentery.
" E.R. HARRIS, 1st Kings. — G.S.W. L. Leg.
" W.M. HUTCHINSON, 1st Kings — G.S.W. R. Thigh.
" A.K. FRASER 4th Seaforth Hdrs. — Influenza.
Major C.S. LEWIS, A.S.C. 1st Div. Train — Rheumatism.

A.D.M.S. 2nd Div.
11/4/15

A. Armstrong
Capt. R.A.M.C.
O.C. No. 4 Field Amb.

No 4 Field Ambulance.

Evacuation Return 11/4/15 9am.

   Lying – 2
   Sitting – 1

  Officer –
   Lying – 1.

    R.H. Lloyd Jones
    Capt. R.A.M.C.
   OC No 4 Field Amb=

OC No. 7 M.A.C

No 4 Field Ambulance
    "

Evacuation Return 3pm.
    "

Officers 2.

other Ranks Lying 3
            Sitting 3
            H M Lockett
                  7th Kame

O.6 Noy Motor Convoy 3
    11-24-15   3
                    3

                    Capt RAMC
                  for O.6 No 4 Fd Ambl

Army Form C. 2118.

WAR DIARY
or
INTELLIGENCE SUMMARY.
(Erase heading not required.)

Instructions regarding War Diaries and Intelligence Summaries are contained in F. S. Regs., Part II. and the Staff Manual respectively. Title pages will be prepared in manuscript.

Hour, Date, Place	Summary of Events and Information	Remarks and references to Appendices
12th April, 1915. BETHUNE.	Our Advanced Trenches having been shelled 11 casualties from 1st Irish Guards were admitted. Number of casualties - 33 Lieut. A.C. Jepson R.A.M.C. (Recommitted to Camerhill) Trans'd by Lieut. Hunter Cantrell, 1st K.R.R. (Senile Decline) No. 7 M.A.C. 2nd Lts. M.P. Bighteen, 2nd Bedfords. Returned to duty. " " C. Jepson 2nd Worcesters " " "	PMO

No 4 Field Ambulance.

No. of Sick & wounded, by Units, admitted during 24 hours ended 9.0 am 12/4/15.

Units :- 2nd Division.	Officers Sick	Officers Wndd	Other Ranks Sick	Other Ranks Wndd	Remarks
2nd. Worcesters	-	-	-	1	To duty :-
2nd South Staffs.	-	-	4	-	R.G.A 35th H.Bty. - 2.
M. M. G. Service	-	-	1	-	
8th Kings.	-	-	2	-	
R.E. 11th Field Coy.	-	-	1	-	
R.F.A. 56th Bty 44th Bge.	-	-	1	-	
2nd. Grenadier Gds.	-	-	-	1	
7th Motor Ambulance Convoy	-	-	1	-	
	-	-	10	2	
Other Divisions :-					Light Duty :-
19th County of London	-	-	1	-	R.A.M.C - 1
20th -do-	-	-	-	1	R.F.A. - 2
1st Black Watch	-	1	-	-	8th Kings - 1
5th London R.F.A.	1	-	-	-	1st Herts - 1
					1st Gren. Gds. 1
	1	1	1	1	

Prevailing disease — Nil
No. admitted with Foot troubles — Nil.

	Sick	Wndd
Admitted Officers	1	1
" Other Rks.	11	3
Evac. Officers	3	1
" Other Rks.	18	6
Remaining Officers	14	3
" Other Rks.	23	15

Evac. by M.A.C :-
  Officers - 3
  Other Ranks - 9
Rest. to duty :-
  Officers - 1
  Other Ranks - 2
Rest. to light duty :-
  Other Ranks - 6.

Officers admitted :

| 1st Black Watch | 2nd/Lt R. I. MACKENZIE | Shell wnd Head. |
| 5th London R.F.A. | Lieut. A. E. SHUTER | Contused wnd Head / accident |

P. A. Lloyd Jones
Capt. R.A.M.C.
O.C. No 4 Field Amb.

A.D.M.S.
  2nd Div.

No 4 Field Ambulance

Evacuation Return 3/pm

Officers 1

Other Ranks Lying 5
            Sitting 5

Bourne Price
Lieut
for Capt RAMC
O.C. No 4 Fd Ambl

O.C. No 4 Motor Convoy
12-4-15

WAR DIARY
or
INTELLIGENCE SUMMARY.
(Erase heading not required.)

Army Form C. 2118.

Instructions regarding War Diaries and Intelligence Summaries are contained in F.S. Regs., Part II. and the Staff Manual respectively. Title pages will be prepared in manuscript.

Hour, Date, Place	Summary of Events and Information	Remarks and references to Appendices
13th April, 1915. BETHUNE.	Lieut. N.M. Cockcroft, R.A.M.C. proceeded today for temporary duty with 1st King's Liverpool Regt. at No. 1 Horley Street. Lieut. T Bourne Price R.A.M.C. proceeded today for temporary duty to 34th Bde. R.F.A. Number of Casualties — 16 2nd Lt. T.C. Campbell, 2nd Black Watch (Rheumatic Fever) " N.K. Fraser, 4th Seaforths (Influenza) Evacuated by No. 7 M.A.C. Capt. M.N.F. Cotton, 6th London. 2nd Lt. F.H. Dickinson, 6th London. } Returned to duty. Capt. S. Martin, R.A.M.C.	[signature]

No 4 Field Ambulance.

No. of Sick & wounded, by Units, admitted during 24 hours ended 9.0 a.m. 13/4/15.

Units. 2nd Division	OFFICERS		OTHER RANKS		Remarks.
	Sick	Wounded	Sick	Wounded	
A.C.C.	-	-	3	-	To duty :-
2nd 5th Staffs att. R.E 170 Coy.	-	-	-	1	2nd 5th Staffs - 1.
2nd Colds. Gds	-	-	4	2	
2nd H.L.I.	-	-	3	-	
1st Irish Gds.	-	-	5	11	
9th H.L.I.	-	-	1	-	
26th Hvy Bty R.G.A.	-	-	1	-	
1st Kings	-	-	-	1	
1st Herts.	-	-	-	1	
Total	-	-	13	16	
Other Divisions :-					Light Duty :-
15th County of London	-	-	-	1	2nd 5th Staffs - 1.
17th -do-	-	-	1	-	
20th -do-	-	-	1	-	
1st Camerons Hdrs	1	-	1	1	
Total.	1	-	2	1	

Prevailing disease — Caries Dentium
No admitted with Foot troubles — Nil

Evacd by M.A.C. :-
Officers — 2
Other Ranks — 9
Retd. to Duty :-
Officers — 2
Other Ranks — 1
Retd to Light duty :-
Other Ranks — 1

		Sick	Wounded
admitted	Officers	1	-
"	Other Rks.	15	17
Evacd.	Officers	4	1
"	Other Rks	7	4
Remaining	Officers	12	3
"	Other Rks.	30	28

Officers admitted

Capt. D.M. Crichton, 1 Cameron Hdrs. Malaria.

P.A. Lord Jones
Capt. R. AMC.
O.C. No 4 Field Amb.

A.D.M.S.
2nd. Div. 12/4/15.

RETURNS
To 24-4-15

No 4 Field Ambulance

Evacuation Return 3pm

Officers. 2

Other Ranks Lying. 4
Sitting. 4

To No 4 Motor Convoy 3
13-4-15

David W Murphy
Lieut
for Capt Rutt A.C
OC No 4 Fd Ambl

Army Form C. 2118.

WAR DIARY
or
INTELLIGENCE SUMMARY.
(Erase heading not required.)

Hour, Date, Place	Summary of Events and Information	Remarks and references to Appendices
14th April, 1915 BETHUNE	Number of Casualties - 19. 2nd Lt A.J. Connor, Corps of Signallers (Reserve) } Evac'd Major P.W. Bereford, 3rd London, (Imperial) } by No 7 " C.N. Fouche, R.E. (Pates). } T.A.C. 2nd Lt E.P.M. Morley, 4th London } Returned to duty. " N.M. Hutcheson 1st Kings } Lieut N.N.P. Morton, R.A.M.C. returned from temporary duty with 44th Bde. R.F.A. No 7013 Pte G. Lawrence, 7th Hussars attached No. 4 Field Ambce on return to Rm H.J. Fleming, proceeded to Boulogne for duty at the Royal Aircraft Factory, Aldershot. No 5050 Cpl. Birtwistle W., R.A.M.C. sent to leave Boulogne for duty in relief of No.3156 Cpl Davies T., R.A.M.C.	

No 4. Field Ambulance.

Evacuation Return 3pm

Officers :- 1
Other Ranks. Lying. 4
                Sitting. 2

O.C. No 1 Motor Convoy
14-4-15

A.y H Lovell
Lieut
for Capt R.A.M.C
O.C. No 4 Field Ambulance

Army Form C. 2118.

WAR DIARY
or
INTELLIGENCE SUMMARY.
(Erase heading not required.)

Hour, Date, Place	Summary of Events and Information	Remarks and references to Appendices
15th April, 1915 BETHUNE.	Lieut N.M. Cockcroft, R.A.M.C. returned from temporary duty with 1st King's Liverpool Regt. Lieut. N.C. Woodyatt, R.A.M.C. arrived for duty from No 18 General Hospital. Number of Casualties - 21. Lieut Anderson Conture, 1st K.R.R. (Cancer Dentume) Evac Capt. A Macfarlane, 2nd Rl. Welsh (Jaundice) by " F.C. Bewsey, 20th City of London (Rheumathma) No.7 " G.M. Fraser, 4th Seaforths (G.S.W. Head) M.A.C. 2nd Lt. E.N. Wixom 23rd London (" ") Lieut. H.E. Shicker, 5th London R.F.A. returned to duty.	

No. 4 Field Ambulance

No. of sick & wounded, by Units, admitted during 24 hours ended 9 a.m. 15/4/15.

Units – 2nd Divsn.	Officers		Other Ranks		Remarks
	Sick	Wond'd	Sick	Wond'd	
2nd Gren. Gds.	-	-	2	1	Duty :-
A.C.C.	-	-	3	-	7th M.A.C. - 1
A.S.C.	-	-	1	-	
3rd Colds Gds.	-	-	3	-	
R.E. 11th Coy.	-	-	1	-	
1st Kings	1	-	-	-	
1st Berks	1	-	1	-	
R.F.A. 35th Bty.	-	-	-	-	
Total	2	-	10	1	
Other Divisions:-					Light Duty:-
18th County of London	-	-	1	-	5th Kings - 2
20th -do-	1	-	1	-	3rd Colds Gds. - 1
15th -do-	-	-	-	-	2nd S. Staffs - 2
4th Seaforth Hdrs	-	1	-	-	R.E. 11 Coy. - 1
23rd County of London	-	1	-	-	20th London - 1
					15th - 1
Total	1	2	2	-	

Prevailing disease – Nil.
No. admitted with Foot Trouble – 1

		Sick	Wond'd
Admitted	Officers	4	2
-"-	Other Ranks	13	1
Evac'd	Officers	4	1
-"-	Other Ranks	10	6
Remaining	Officers	10	4
-"-	Other Ranks	20	3

Evac'd by M.A.C.:-
Officers – 3
Other Ranks – 7
Ret'd to Duty:-
Officers – 2
Other Ranks – 1
Ret'd to Light Duty:-
Other Ranks – 8

Officers admitted. 14/4/15.
Capt. F.C. BENTLEY   20th London Regt.   Neurasthenia
Capt. G.W. FRASER   4th Seaforth Hdrs.   G.S.W. Head
Major C.H. FOULKES   R.E. 11th Field Coy. Piles
Lieut. E.R. LAST   1st Kings.   Contused Wd. Hand
  "   J.H. WOODS   1st R. Berks   N.Y.D.
2nd Lt. E.N. NIXON   23 County of London Bullet wd. Head slight.

P.H. Lloyd Jones
Capt. R.A.M.C.
O.C. No. 4 Field Amb.

a. D.M.S.
2nd Divs. 15/4/15.

No 4 Field Ambulance

Evacuation Return 3pm

Officers 5.

Others Ranks Lying 8
           Sitting 5

O.b. Noy Motor Convoy. }   H Morton Lieut.
      15-4-15   }   for Capt R A M C
                       }   O.b. No 4 Fd Ambl

WAR DIARY
or
INTELLIGENCE SUMMARY.

(Erase heading not required.)

Army Form C. 2118.

Hour, Date, Place	Summary of Events and Information	Remarks and references to Appendices
April 14th. 1915 BETHUNE.	Rev. P.N. Waggett, proceeded to No. 4 Casualty Clearing Station, for duty. No. 11817 Pte Speed, 2nd Grenadier Guards, attached No. 4 Field Ambce. as batman to Rev P.N. Waggett, proceeded to No.4 Casualty Clearing Station for duty. Lieut T. Bourne - Price RAMC informed that, "Under instructions from A.D.M.S., 2nd Divn you have been transferred from this Unit to No. 6 Field Ambulance from 15th. instant." Number of Casualties - 25. Lieut A.J. Bowles, 1st R. Berks. returned to duty.	PKD

No 4 Field Ambulance

Evacuation Return 3pm

Other Ranks Lying 1
             Sitting 16 17 B.M.M

(one extra for evacuation added after
list had been completed) B.M.M
                        Basil M Murphy

O.C. No 4 Motor Convoy   Lieut
   16.4.15   for Capt B AMC
                        OC No 4 Fd Amb

No 4 Field Ambulance.

No. of sick, wounded, by Units, admitted during 24 hours ended 9.0 am. 16/4/15.

Units – 2nd Divn.	Officers Sick	Officers Wndd	Other Ranks Sick	Other Ranks Wndd	Remarks
2nd Grenadier Gds	–	–	–	2	To duty:–
2nd Inniskilling Fusrs	–	–	1	1	
R.E. 2nd Signal Coy.	–	–	1	–	Nil.
3rd Coldstream Gds	–	–	3	–	
2nd —do—	–	–	2	–	
1st H.L.R.	–	–	1	1	
1st Kings.	–	–	1	–	
1st R. Berks.	1	–	–	–	
7th Kings.	–	–	3	–	
2nd Worcesters	1	–	–	1	
R.E. 1st East Anglian	–	–	–	–	
Total	2	–	13	4	
Other Divisions:–					To Light duty:–
15th City of London	–	–	–	2	2nd R. W. F. – 1
17th —do—	–	–	–	1	1 Herts – 1
					A.C.C. – 1
Total	2	–	–	–	

Prevailing disease – Caries Dentis
No admitted with Foot troubles – Nil

Evacd by M.A.C:–
Officers – 4
Other Ranks – 15

Retd to Duty:–
Officers – 1
Other Ranks – Nil

Retd to Light duty:–
Other Ranks – 3

		Sick	Wndd
Admitted	Officers	2	–
—"—	Other Ranks	13	7
Evacd	Officers	3	2
—"—	Other Ranks	11	7
Remaining	Officers	9	2
—"—	Other Ranks	22	3

Officers admitted
1st Berks. Lt A. J. BOWLES. R.I. Hernia
R.E (1st East Ang) 2nd Lt E. T. BRADDELL. Influenza.

P. H. Lloyd Jones
Capt. R.A.M.C.
O.C. No 4 Field Amb

A.D.M.S
2nd Div. 16/4/15.

Army Form C. 2118.

WAR DIARY
or
INTELLIGENCE SUMMARY.
(Erase heading not required.)

Instructions regarding War Diaries and Intelligence Summaries are contained in F. S. Regs., Part II. and the Staff Manual respectively. Title pages will be prepared in manuscript.

Hour, Date, Place	Summary of Events and Information	Remarks and references to Appendices
17th April, 1915. BETHUNE	Casualties — 35. Lieut. R. Shaw. 7th Kings (P.U.O Fever) } Evac'd " E. M. Campbell. RAMC (N.Y.& Throat) } by No 7 M.A.C. Capt. R. M. Mitchell, 2nd Lancs Fus. } Returned to Lieut. B. Scott, RAMC } duty " E. R. Lash, 1st Kings " J. N. Woods, 1st R Berks.	OK B/

No 4 Field Ambulance

No. of Sick & wounded, by Units, admitted during 24 hours ended 9.0 am 17/4/15.

Units - 2nd Divn.	Officers		Other Ranks		Remarks.
	Sick	Wondd.	Sick	Wondd.	
2nd. Grenadier Gds.	.	.	.	1	To Duty :-
2nd South Staffs	.	.	1	.	
RAMC (Sanitary Sect).	.	.	1	.	1st Berks. 1 Officer
7th Kings	1	.	5	.	19th C. of L. 1
2nd. Worcesters	.	.	1	.	
1st Herts	.	.	2	2	
1st Irish Gds	.	.	1	.	
2nd Colds. Gds.	.	.	1	.	
2nd Kings R'oals.	.	.	1	1	
R.F.A. 2nd D. Art.	.	.	.	.	
	1	.	13	4	
Other Divisions:					
14th City of London	.	.	2	.	To Light Duty :-
20th - do -	.	.	3	.	
R.A.M.C. att. R.M.F.	.	.	.	.	Nil
5th Sussex	1	.	.	.	
Total	2	.	5	.	

Prevailing disease - Caries Dent.
No admitted with Foot troubles - one

Evacd. by M.A.C :-
  Officers - Nil
  Other Ranks - 18
Retd. to Duty :
  Officers - 1
  Other Ranks - 1
Retd to Light duty :-
  Other Ranks - Nil

		Sick	Wondd.
Admitted	Officers	3	.
"	Other Ranks	18	4
Evacuated	Officers	1	.
"	Other Ranks	18	1
Remaining	Officers	1	2
"	Other Ranks	22	6

Officers admitted
7th Kings   Lt R. SHAW,   N.y.D.
R.A.M.C. att. 2nd Munsters, Lt CAMPBELL G.M. Pharyngitis
5th Sussex.   2nd Lt. A.R.M. Dodd.   Concussion

P. A. Lloyd Jones
Capt. R.A.M.C.
O.C. No 4 Field Amb

A.D.M.S.
2nd Div. 17/4/15.

No 4 Field Ambulance

Evacuation Return 3pm

Other Ranks Lying   6
          Sitting   6

O.C. No 4 Motor Convoy
3pm 17-4-15

T S Manson
Capt R.A.M.C
for O.C. No 4 Field Amb

Army Form C. 2118.

WAR DIARY
or
INTELLIGENCE SUMMARY.
(Erase heading not required.)

Instructions regarding War Diaries and Intelligence Summaries are contained in F.S. Regs., Part II. and the Staff Manual respectively. Title pages will be prepared in manuscript.

Hour, Date, Place	Summary of Events and Information	Remarks and references to Appendices
18th April, 1915 BETHUNE	The A.D.M.S. 2nd London Division and his Staff Officers visited the Dressing Station. The G.O.C. 2nd Division and the A.D.M.S. 2nd Division also visited the Dressing Station. No. 5356, Pte. J. Short, R.A.M.C. proceeded to duty with South Irish Horse at Maker Curb Orchard. Number of casualties – 22 2nd Lieut. G.T.N. Frowde 1st K.R.R. (Shell-wound Reg.) Force's " " C. Tyars, 2nd Worcesters (Jaundice) by No. 7 F.A.C. Capt. Bryn Crichton 1st Camerons returned to duty.	

No 4 Field Ambulance

N° of sick & wounded, by Units, admitted during 24 hours ended 9-0 a.m. 18/4/15.

Units - 2nd Div.	Officers Sick	Officers Wnd'd	Other Ranks Sick	Other Ranks Wnd'd	Remarks
R.F.A. 2nd D.A.C.	-	-	1	-	To duty:-
R.E. 2nd Signal Coy	-	-	1	-	
2nd South Staffs.	-	-	2	9	2nd Colds. Gds. - 1
M.M.G. Sect 1st Batn	-	-	1	-	3rd do - 1
R.F.A. 34 Bde H.Q. Staff	-	-	1	-	2nd Gren. Gds. 1 Officer
1st Herts	-	-	1	7	R. Ame. 1 -
3rd Coldstream Gds.	-	-	1	2	1st Kings 1 -
R.F.A. 3rd Mountain Howd. Bty	-	-	1	-	1st Berks 1 -
1st Irish Gds.	-	-	1	-	
7th Kings	-	-	1	-	
2nd Grenadier Gds.	-	-	1	1	
1st K.R.R.	-	1	-	1	
1st R. Berks	-	-	-	1	
2nd H.L.I.	-	-	-	1	
Total	-	1	11	20	

Other Divisions:					
1st South Wales Bdrs	2	-	-	-	To light duty:-
2nd A.I.D.	-	-	-	1	do. - 1.
Total	2	-	-	1	

Prevailing disease. — Nil
N° admitted with Foot troubles. — Nil

Evac'd by M.A.C.:
- Officers — 2
- Other Ranks — 13

Rel'd to duty:-
- Officers — 4
- Other Ranks — 2

Rel'd to light duty:-
- Other Ranks — 1

		Sick	Wnd'd
Admitted	Officers	2	1
"	Other Ranks	11	20
Evac'd	Officers	6	-
"	Other Ranks	10	6
Remaining	Officers	7	3
"	Other Ranks	23	20

Officers Admitted.
1st South Wales Bdrs — Capt. R.S. GWYNN, Lumbago
— do — 2nd/Lt. C. MUMFORD Constipation
1st. K.R.R. 2nd Lt. G.F.H. FRANCE Shell Wd. L. Thigh

P.A. Christopher
Capt. R.A.M.C.
Act.O/C 4 Field Amb.

A.D.M.S.
2nd Div.
18/4/15.

No 4 Field Ambulance
       "

Evacuation Return. 3 pm
    "

Officers ?
Other Ranks. Lying: 4.
            Sitting: 4.

O.C. No4 Motor Convoy }   HMLockeroft Lieut. Ram
    18.4.-15   }   for Capt R.A.M.C.
                      }   O.C. No 4 Field Amb

Army Form C. 2118.

WAR DIARY
or
INTELLIGENCE SUMMARY.
(Erase heading not required.)

Instructions regarding War Diaries and Intelligence Summaries are contained in F.S. Regs., Part II. and the Staff Manual respectively. Title pages will be prepared in manuscript.

Hour, Date, Place	Summary of Events and Information	Remarks and references to Appendices
19th April, 1915 BETHUNE.	Lieut. N.H.P. Morton, R.A.M.C. proceeds for temporary duty to 2nd Heavy Brigade R.G.A. Rev. Buxton Gwynne (Bishop of Khartoum) joined for duty. 2 Colonels (R.A.M.C. T) posted to this unit for purpose of instruction and observation as to methods of working of a Field Ambulance. No. of Casualties - 44 2nd Lt. H.R.M. Dodd, 5th R Sussex returned to duty. No. 5051 Pte J. Povey, R.A.M.C. (now to Amb.) evacuated to Base.	

No 4 Field Ambulance

Evacuation Return 3pm.

Other Ranks: Lying: – 5
             Sitting: – 8

OC No 4 Motor Convoy   David D Humphrey
19-4-15   Lt RAMC
                         for Capt R.t N6
                         OC No 4 Fd Ambl.

No. 4 Field Ambulance

No. of sick & wounded by Units admitted during 24 hours ended 9.0 am 19/4/18.

Units – 2nd Divn	Officers		Other Ranks		Remarks
	Sick	Wound	Sick	Wound	
2nd H.L.I.	–	–	–	1	To duty:–
M.G.G.Servs	–	–	2	1	No
2nd South Staffs	–	–	4	1	1 Cameron Hdrs.
1st R. Berks	–	–	1	–	1 Officer (L.rank)
3rd Coldstream Gds	–	–	1	2	
2nd Grenadier Gds	–	–	1	–	
7th Kings	–	–	–	1	
R.F.A. 56th Bty	–	–	1	–	
2nd Worcesters	1	–	–	–	
South Irish Horse	1	–	–	–	
	2	–	10	5	

Other Divisions					To Light Duty
15th C. of London	–	–	1	–	1st Herts – 1
19th –do–	–	–	1	–	Queens Gds – 1
23rd –do–	1	–	–	–	3rd Colds Gds – 1
6th –do–	2	–	–	–	
	3	–	2	–	

Evacd by M.A.C.
Officers 2
Other Ranks 11

Retd to Duty
Officers 1
Other Ranks –

Retd to Light Duty
Other Ranks 3

			Sick	Wound
Admitted	Officers		5	–
"	Other Ranks		12	5
Evacd	Officers		2	1
"	Other Ranks		5	9
Remaining	Officers		10	2
"	Other Ranks		30	16

Officers Admitted
6th London Regt. Lt. T.W. WARDHAUGH   Myalgia
    "   2nd Lt. J.G. GREGORY Piles
2nd Worcesters   2nd Lt. C. FYSON   Jaundice
South Irish Horse Lt. F.H. BROOKE   Pleurodynia
23rd London Regt. Lt. C.A.C. ROWLEY   Influenza

P. A. Lloyd Jones
Capt. R.A.M.C.
O.C. No 4 Field Amb.

A.D.M.S. 2nd Divn

Army Form C. 2118.

WAR DIARY
or
INTELLIGENCE SUMMARY.
(Erase heading not required.)

Instructions regarding War Diaries and Intelligence Summaries are contained in F.S. Regs., Part II. and the Staff Manual respectively. Title pages will be prepared in manuscript.

Hour, Date, Place	Summary of Events and Information	Remarks and references to Appendices
20th April, 1915. BETHUNE.	Commanding Officers inspected the Advanced Dressing Stations at PONT FIXE. Number of Casualties – 32. Capt. R.S Guynan, 1st S.M.B., (Myalgia) 2nd Lt. C. Mumford, 1st S.W.B., (Contusion) " A.B Playford, 2nd S.M.B. (G.S.W. R. Hand) Capt. E.B Henderson, 2nd Bd. Watch (Shell wd. Shr & Arm) " H Ramsden, R.F.A. (Deafness) Lt. Col. Priestley, 22nd London, 2nd Lt. E.T Bradfield, R.E (East Anglian)	} Evac'd by No 7 M.A.C } Returned to duty.

No 4 Field Ambulance

Sick & wounded, by Units, admitted during
24 hours ended 9:30am 20/4/18.

Units - 2nd Div	Officers		Other Ranks		Remarks
	Sick	Wnd	Sick	Wndd	
2nd South Staffs	-	-	4	-	To duty:-
5th Kings	-	-	1	-	2nd South Staffs - 1
7th Kings	-	-	4	-	
2nd Grenadier Gds	-	-	4	-	5th Sussex - 1 Officer
R.Fd. 7th Bty	-	-	1	-	
R.F.a. 9rd Bty	-	-	1	-	
9th Bde.	-	-	1	-	
R.E. 11th Coy	-	-	-	1	
3rd Colds. Gds.	-	-	-	1	
R.A.M.C. 4 Fd Amb.	-	-	1	-	
1st Herts	-	-	2	1	
	-	-	17	3	
Other Divisions:					To Light Duty:-
20th London Regt	-	-	1	-	
6th - do -	-	-	20	-	1st Herts - 1
3rd South Wales Bdrs	-	1	-	-	R.F.a. 26 Bty - 1
2nd Black Watch	-	1	-	-	7th Kings - 1
17th London Regt	-	-	-	1	20th London - 1
	-	2	21	1	

Prevailing disease - Diarrhoea
No. admitted with Foot troubles - 4

		Sick	Wndd
Evacd. by M.A.C.	Admitted Officers	-	2
Officers Nil	Other Ranks	38	4
Other Ranks 7	Evacuated Officers	1	-
R.P. to Duty	Other Ranks	16	3
Officers - 1	Remaining Officers	2	4
Other Ranks - 1	Other Ranks	52	17
R.P. to Light Duty			
Other Ranks - 4			

Officers Admitted

3rd South Wales Bdrs — 2nd Lieut. A.B. PLAYFORD — G.S.W. Rt Hand
2nd Black Watch — Capt. C.B. HENDERSON — Shell wnd Rt Ear & Rt Shoulder

P.H. Lloyd Jones
Capt. R.A.M.C.
O.C. No 4 Field Amb.

A.D.M.S. 2nd Div.
9 am 20/4/18.

No 4 Field Ambulance.
    "   "

Evacuation Return 9 am

Other Ranks Lying = 4
              Sitting NIL

                    BasilTMurphy.
                        Lieut
O No 4 Motor Convoy   for Capt R A M C
20.4-15   O.C No 4 Fd Amb.

Army Form C. 2118.

WAR DIARY
or
INTELLIGENCE SUMMARY.
(Erase heading not required.)

Instructions regarding War Diaries and Intelligence Summaries are contained in F.S. Regs., Part II. and the Staff Manual respectively. Title pages will be prepared in manuscript.

Hour, Date, Place	Summary of Events and Information	Remarks and references to Appendices
21st April, 1915. BETHUNE.	Chaplain Rector Gwynne proceeded to No. 5 Field Ambulance for duty. Chaplain C.F. Baines joined for duty from No. 6 Field Ambulance. No. 8888 Pte H. Bourne, R.A.M.C. and No. 308 Pte H. Bond 3.D. Hussars proceed to No. 5 Field Ambulance for duty as Batman & Groom to Chaplain Bishop Gwynne. Number of Casualties - 28. Major The Hon. C.H.B. Willoughby, M.P., 1st Coldstream Guards admitted officers' Dressing Station with Influenza.	

(73989) W4141—463. 400,000. 9/14. H.&J.Ltd. Forms/C. 2118/10.

"WAR DIARY" or "INTELLIGENCE SUMMARY."

Hour, Date, Place	Summary of Events and Information	Remarks and references to Appendices
22nd April, 1915. BETHUNE.	The following is a copy of an order received from Adv'd. 2nd Div'n. Secret. M.D. 551. O.C. 1/5 Field Ambulance. 22. Re Extract operation order 2nd Div'n. 35. 21/4/15. 4 Field Ambulance will take over the evacuation of the CUINCHY Section in addition to the GIVENCHY Section from 10 a.m. 24th April and will remain under London Div'n to evacuate area held by 4th (Guards) Brigade. London Div'n will take over the evacuation of the FESTUBERT Section from 10 a.m. 25th April on which the advanced portions of 5 Field Ambulance will be withdrawn to BETHUNE. (Signed) M.A. Hood.	

No. 4 Field Ambulance

Return of Sick & wounded by Units, admitted during 24 hours ended 9.0 am 21/4/15.

Unit - 2nd Div.	Officers Sick	Officers Wndd	Other Ranks Sick	Other Ranks Wndd	Remarks
1st Herts.	.	2	4	4	To Duty:-
1st Irish Gds.	.	.	2	-	2nd Sth Staffs - 1
A.S.C. 2nd Div.	.	.	1	-	5th Kings - 1
2nd Coldstream Gds.	.	.	2	1	R.M.G.S. - 1
R.G.A. 35th H. Bty	.	.	4	-	6th London - 1
1st Berks.	.	.	1	-	
2nd Grenadier Gds.	.	.	2	.	
A.S.C. 10th Coy.	.	.	1	-	
R.F.A. 70th Bat.	.	.	.	1	
M.M.G. Service 1 Bn.	.	.	1	.	
R.F.A. 41st Bde. A.C.	1	.	.	.	
Total	**1**	**2**	**18**	**6**	
Other Divisions:-					To Light Duty:-
6th London Regt.	.	.	.	1	R.F.A. 34th B. - 1
7th -do-	.	.	2	.	2nd South Staffs - 3
8th -do-	.	.	2	.	1st Irish Gds. - 1
1st R.I. Fus.	.	.	1	.	3rd Coldstream Gds. - 1
~~R.A.M.C (5th London)~~					1st Herts - 1
8th London Regt.	.	.	1	.	R.A.M.C. - 1
~~-do-~~					9th City of London - 1
Total	.	.	**6**	**1**	

Prevailing disease - Shock
N° admitted with out troubles - Nil.

Evacd by M.A.C:-
 Officers - 5
 Other Ranks - 11
Retd to Light Duty
 Other Ranks - 9
Retd. to Duty
 Officers - 2
 Other Ranks - 4

			Sick	Wndd.
Admitted	Officers		1	2
-"-	Other Ranks		34	7
Evacuated	Officers		5	2
-"-	Other Ranks		16	8
Remaining	Officers		5	4
-"-	Other Ranks		60	16

Officers admitted.
1st Herts   Capt. E. LONGMORE   Concussion (wound)
  -"-   Lieut. A.G. BORWICK   -"-
R.F.A. 41 Bde Amc. Capt. H. RAMSDEN   Deafness.

P. A. Short Jones
Capt. RAMC
O.C. N° 4 Fld Amb.

ADms. 5
2nd Div. 21/4/15

No 4 Field Ambulance.

Evacuation Return 3 pm

Other Ranks Lying :- 4.
               Sitting :- 15.

O.C. No 4 Motor Convoy
21-4-15.

M. Watt
Capt R.A.M.C.
O.C. No 4 Field Amb.

WAR DIARY
or
INTELLIGENCE SUMMARY.
(Erase heading not required.)

Army Form C. 2118.

Hour, Date, Place	Summary of Events and Information	Remarks and references to Appendices
22nd April, 1915 BETHUNE. (Continued)	The D.D.M.S. Army, inspected the Officers' Dressing Station. Number of Casualties – 19. Lieut. F. N. Brooke, South Irish Horse (N.Y.S. Regiment) 2nd Lt. H. R. Bromley-Smith, Interpreter, att. 9th Batt. R.F.A. } (Mesopotamia) Lieut. H. H. Pollock, 13th London R.F.N. (Machine Tikras) Evacuated by No. 7 M.A.C. Capt. E. Kengrove, 1st Herts. } Returned to duty. Lieut. R. G. Barwick, 1st Herts. }	

No. 4 Field Ambulance.

No. of sick & wounded, by Units, admitted during 24 hours 9. a.m. 22/4/15.

Unit – 2nd Div	Officers Sick	Officers Wond'd	Other Ranks Sick	Other Ranks Wond'd	Remarks
2nd Irish Gds.	.	.	1	.	To duty:-
5th Kings	.	.	2	.	2nd South Staffs – 1
R.F.A. A.C.	.	.	1	.	M.M.G.S. – 2
A.C.C. Div.	.	.	2	.	2nd Coldstream Gds – 1
R.E. 31st Coy.	.	.	3	.	1. R. I. Fus. – 1.
R.G.A. 35th H.Bty.	.	.	1	.	6th London – 6
2nd Coldstream Gds.	.	.	.	1	
2nd South Staffs	.	.	.	1	
1st Irish Gds.	.	.	2	.	
Total	.	.	12	3	

Other Divisions:					
8th London Regt.	.	.	2	.	To Light Duty:-
7th -do-	.	.	.	.	
R.E. 1st Coy. (London)	.	.	.	.	1st. R. Berks – 1
6th London Regt.	.	.	1	4	2nd South Staff – 1
7th London R.F.A.	.	.	1	.	2nd Irish Gds – 1
5th London Bde 12Bty R.F.A.	1	.	.	.	7th Kings – 1
4th R. Welsh Fus.	1	.	.	.	16th London – 1
Interpreter attd. 84 Bty R.F.A. Lahore Div.	1	.	.	.	
1st Coldstream Gds.	1	.	.	.	
Total	4	.	6	4	

Prevailing disease – Inf. of Bowels.

Evac'd by M.A.C.
Officers –
Other Ranks 20

Ret'd to Duty
Officers –
Other Ranks 11

Ret'd to Light duty
Other Ranks – 5

No. admitted with Foot troubles – 1

		Sick	Wond'd
Admitted	Officers	4	–
"	Other Ranks	18	6
Evacuated	Officers	–	–
"	Other Ranks	34	2
Remaining	Officers	9	4
	Other Ranks	44	20

Admitted Officers.

4th R. Welsh Fus. Capt. F. B. CLOUGH. Diarrhoea
2nd Lt. Interpreter attchd 84th Bat R.F.A. Lahore Div 2nd Lt. H.R. BROMLEY SMITH. Neurasthenia
1st Coldstream Gds. Major The Hon. C.H.D. WILLOUGHBY M.P. Influenza.
12th County London R.F.A. Lt. H. H. POLLOCK. Fracture R. Leg.

P. A. Lloyd Jones
Capt. R.A.M.C.
O.C. No. 4 Field Amb.

A.D.M.S.
2nd Div. 22/4/15

No 4 Field Ambulance

Evacuation Return, 9.0.am.

Officers   Nil
Other Ranks. Lying-5.

O.C. No 7 M.A.C.
22/4/15.

H Woodyatt
Lt Name
for Capt. R. AMC.
O.C No 4 Field Amb

No 14. Field Ambulance
—"—

Evacuation Return 3pm
—"—

Officers 3

Other Ranks: Lying 5.
            Sitting 6.

M.O. i/c
 7 Motor Convoy
 22-4-15

H Holdsworth Lt
for Capt RAMC
O.C. No 4 F.d Amb

WAR DIARY
INTELLIGENCE SUMMARY

(Erase heading not required.)

Army Form C. 2118.

Hour, Date, Place	Summary of Events and Information	Remarks and references to Appendices
23rd April, 1915. BETHUNE.	Capt. T.S. Blackwell, R.A.M.C. proceeded to England for duty. The following is a copy of the orders issued to Capt. T.S. Blackwell R.A.M.C.:— "Under instructions from No.1 1st Army, you will proceed to England for duty with the Territorial reporting at War Office on arrival, vide War Office letter No. 121/7/Divns/583 (A.M.B.1) of 11/4/15". Lieut. H.C. Woodyatt, R.A.M.C. proceeded for duty to 2nd Coldstream Guards. The following is a copy of the orders issued to Lieut. H.C. Woodyatt, R.A.M.C.:— "You are posted to LE QUESNOY, tomorrow morning 24th, for duty as M.O. in charge 2nd Coldstream Guards in relief of Capt. T.S. Byas, R.A.M.C." Capt. G.E. Byas, R.A.M.C. arrived for duty from 2nd Coldstream Guards. No. 15196 Sgt. C.T. Pepper, R.A.M.C. arrived for duty from No. 9 Stationary Hospital.	

Army Form C. 2118.

WAR DIARY
or
INTELLIGENCE SUMMARY.
(Erase heading not required.)

Instructions regarding War Diaries and Intelligence Summaries are contained in F. S. Regs., Part II and the Staff Manual respectively. Title pages will be prepared in manuscript.

Hour, Date, Place	Summary of Events and Information	Remarks and references to Appendices
23rd April, 1915 BETHUNE.	Number of Casualties — 32. Major J. M. Mahoney, RAMC. (Pneumonia & Pleurisy) and Capt. T.B. Hornblower, 5th R. Sussex (G.S.W. R. Knee Thumb) were evacuated at 8-30 am direct to the Ambulance Train at CHOCQUES. Capt. Détant Raadifer, 105th Mahrata L.I. attacked 10pm. Baluchis who was to have been evacuated in the same manner was detained at the opened Dressing Station for further treatment.	

No. 4 Field Ambulance

No. of Sick & wounded, by Units, admitted during 24 hours ended 9.am 23/4/18.

Unit - 2nd Div.	Officers		Other Ranks		Remarks
	Sick	Wndd	Sick	Wndd	
2nd South Staffs.	-	2	1	-	To Duty:-
1st Irish Gds.	-	-	2	3	2nd South Staffs - 1
A.S.C. (35th Coy).	-	-	1	-	2nd Colds. Gds - 1
1st Herts.	-	-	1	1	6th London - 4
1st Kings	-	-	1	-	
R.E. (11th Field Coy).	-	-	1	1	
2nd Worcesters	1	-	-	-	
5th Kings	-	-	-	1	
Total	1	2	6	6	
Other Divisions.					To light duty:-
R.E. (31st Coy)	-	-	1	-	2nd South Staffs - 1
1st R.I. Fusls	-	-	1	-	2nd Gren. Gds - 1
8th London Regt.	-	-	-	1	6th London - 8
1st South Wales Bdrs	1	-	-	-	5th " " - 1
Total	1	-	2	1	

Prevailing Disease - Nil
No. admitted with Foot troubles - Nil

Evacd. by M.A.C.
  Officers - 3
  Other Ranks - 17
Retd. to Duty.
  Officers - 2
  Other Ranks - 6
Retd. to Light Duty
  Other Ranks - 11

		Sick	Wndd
Admitted	Officers	2	2
"	Other Ranks	8	7
Evacd.	Officers	3	2
"	Other Ranks	28	6
Remaining	Officers	8	4
"	Other Ranks	24	21

Officers admitted

2nd South Staffs.	Lt. H.C. CHRISTOPHERSON	Shell wnd & Shock
- do -	2nd Lt. S. DOUGLAS WILLAN	Shell wnd Head
2nd Worcesters	2nd Lt. R.V.L. JOHNSTONE	Abscess Neck
1st S. W. Bdrs.	Lt. C.A. BAKER	Influenza

A.D.M.S. 2nd Div.
9.am 23/4/18

P. H. Lloyd Jones
Capt. R. Amc
OC No 4 Field Amb

No 4. Field Ambulance.

Evacuation Return. 3/pm.

Other Ranks. Lying. 8
     Sitting. 13.

O.C. No 4 Motor Convoy.
23. 4. 15

Basil W Murphy
Lieut
for Capt R A M C
O.C. No 4 Field Ambl.

Army Form C. 2118.

WAR DIARY
or
INTELLIGENCE SUMMARY.
(Erase heading not required.)

Instructions regarding War Diaries and Intelligence Summaries are contained in F.S. Regs., Part II. and the Staff Manual respectively. Title pages will be prepared in manuscript.

Hour, Date, Place	Summary of Events and Information	Remarks and references to Appendices
24th April 1915. BETHUNE.	Sir Wilmot Herringham, Consulting Physician to the Forces visited the Officers Dressing Station for the purpose of holding a conversation with the Commanding Officer with regard to Capt Delmé-Radcliffe and Lieut. H. C. Christopherson. The following is a copy of Secret Orders issued to the OC Bearer Sub-Divisions, No. 4 Field Ambulance:- "O.C. Bearer S.D. 4 F.A. **Secret** 1. At 3 p.m. tomorrow, the 25th inst. you will take over the Château and Schools at BEUVRY from a representative of No. 5 Field Ambulance who has received instructions to hand over to you. These buildings will not be given to anyone without reference to me. 2. Sgt. Martin R.A.M.C. and 72 men will meet you at the Schools at BEUVRY at 3 p.m. on 25th inst. 3. Reconduct the men of your personnel as is convenient but send any men back to BETHUNE that you find surplus to requirements. 4. Distribution of Officers and N.C.Os. No other officers can be allowed you for the present. If no officers are posted at the Advanced Dressing Station Sgt. Halcrowe should be posted to Pont Fixe and Sgt. Moring to the Château as now done. This suggests that Sgt. Martin	

Army Form C. 2118.

WAR DIARY
or
INTELLIGENCE SUMMARY.
(Erase heading not required.)

Instructions regarding War Diaries and Intelligence Summaries are contained in F.S. Regs., Part II. and the Staff Manual respectively. Title pages will be prepared in manuscript.

Hour, Date, Place	Summary of Events and Information	Remarks and references to Appendices
24th April, 1915 BETHUNE. (Continued)	being sent to the work of the Bearer Divisions should be placed to the killed in BEUVRY. 5. Two horsed ambulance wagons will be sent to you at BEUVRY at 3pm tomorrow 25th instant, and should be taken on your charge there." (Signed) F.R. Layfgones Capt. RAMC O.C. No 4 to Ambce Commanding Officers visited the Advanced Dressing Station and found the above orders had been carried out and everything proceeding as hitherto. Number of Casualties - 43 Capt. F.B. Clough, 4th R.W.F., (Diarrhoea) Evac'd by No. 7 M.A.C. Lieut. T. Douglas Williams, 2nd S. Staffds. } Returned to duty. G.N. Cohen, 5th Kings.	

No 4 Field Ambulance.

No. of sick & wounded, by Unit admitted during 24 hours ended 9 am 24/4/18.

Units. 2nd Div.	Officers Sick	Officers Wnd	Other Ranks Sick	Other Ranks Wnd	Remarks
3rd Coldstream Gds.	.	.	2	.	To duty.
1st K.R.R.	.	.	1	.	R.G.A. 36 H.RBy - 2
1st Irish Gds.	.	.	2	.	Q.C.C. - 1
2nd Coldstream Gds.	.	.	2	.	15th London - 2.
R.F.A (16th Bty).	.	.	1	1	
5th Kings.	.	1	.	.	
R.A.M.C (4 Fd Amb)	.	.	.	1	
Total	.	1	8	2	
Other Divisions:					To Light Duty :-
17th London Regt.	.	.	.	1	
6th -do-	.	.	2	1	2nd Scots Gds - 1
8th -do-	.	1	5	5	70th Bty R.F.a. - 1
R.E. (315th Coy)	.	.	.	.	1st Herts - 5
15th London Regt.	.	.	2	.	2nd 5th Staffs - 1
R.E. (170th Coy)	1	.	.	.	a.C.C - 1
Chaplain attd 2 Munsters	1	.	.	.	7th London R.F.a. 1
25th London Regt.	1	.	.	.	
Total.	3	1	10	7	

Prevailing disease. - Influenza
N° admitted with foot troubles - Nil.

Evactd by M.AC:
Officers 2.
Other Ranks 21.
Retd to Duty
Officers -
Other Ranks 2
Retd to Light duty
Other Ranks 10.

		Sick	Wndd
Admitted	Officers	3	2
"	Other Ranks	18	9
Evacuated	Officers	1	1
"	Other Ranks	23	13
Remaining	Officers	10	5
"	Other Ranks	19	17

Officers admitted

170th Coy. R.E.	2nd Lt. R.W. Williamson	Glass Wnd Chin.
5th Kings.	Lt. G. H. COHEN	Shell wnd Thigh
2nd Munsters.	Chaplain. Rev. Father F.A. GLEESON	Influenza.
8th London.	2/Lt. R. M. MAC CARE	Shell wnd Legs.
25th -do-	Lt. A.L. PALMER	Colic.

P. A. Lloyd Jones
Capt. R. AMC
O.C. N° 4 Field Amb.

A.D.M.S.
2nd Div. 24/4/18

No. 4. Field Ambulance

Evacuation Return 3pm

Officers 1

Other Ranks Lying 4
            Sitting 10

O.C. No 4 Motor Convoy
24 - 4 - 15

[signature]
Capt RAMC
O.C. No 4 Fd Ambl.

Army Form C. 2118.

WAR DIARY
or
INTELLIGENCE SUMMARY.
(Erase heading not required.)

Hour, Date, Place	Summary of Events and Information	Remarks and references to Appendices
25th April, 1915. BETHUNE.	The G.O.C. 2nd Divn. and Staff inspected the Main Dressing Station and the Officers' Dressing Station. The following is a copy of a letter received from Capt. J.J. O'Keefe, R.A.M.C., O/C Bearer Sub-Division, No. 4 Field Ambulance in reply to my Secret Order of yesterday. "I have taken over the Châteaux and Schools at BEUVRY. I am leaving two agents from the detachment previously with Sgt. Martin to assist at our Advanced Dressing Station and I consider it advisable to have an extra one at No.1 Hockley Street, and a similar at PONT FIXE agreed as No.1 Hockley Street, and a similar at PONT FIXE agreed. I am leaving Sgt. Martin, 1 Cpl. Lowe and 3 n.c.o's to posts Schools and Châteaux. I have instructed Sgt. Martin to take in any casualties that may come to the Schools and send forward to you." The Commanding Officer inspected the Schools at BEUVRY and the Châteaux and saw that it was properly fixed over and that 1 Sgt., 1 L/Cpl. and 3 men were in charge. No. 218 Sgt. L.A. Dace, R.A.M.C. proceeded to No.9 Stationary Hospital, Havre, for duty. 2 N.C.O's and 10 men R.A.M.C., 1 N.C.O. and 2 men A.S.C. and 10 Advanced dressing station for duty with Bearer Sub-Division.	

Army Form C. 2118.

WAR DIARY
or
INTELLIGENCE SUMMARY.
(Erase heading not required.)

Hour, Date, Place	Summary of Events and Information	Remarks and references to Appendices
25th April, 1915 BETHUNE. (Continued)	Number of Casualties – 35 Capt. G. H. Childs, Head Quarter Staff, London Divn. admitted Officers Dressing Station suffering from Neurasthenia Lieut A.J. Andrew-Cartwell 1st K.R.R. (Neuralgia and Debility) Capt. B. Longmore, 1st Herts. (Debility) Cross, 2nd Bedfords (for Dental Treatment) Lieut R.G. Bower, 1st Herts. (Debility) Lieut E.L. Kaye, R.A. 2nd Bdg. (Old Injury to Knee) Evacuated by No. 7 M.A.C.	

No. 4 Field Ambulance.

Return shewing number of sick & wounded, by units admitted during 24 hours ended 9 am 25/4/15.

Units - 2nd Div.	Officers		Other Ranks		Remarks
	Sick	Wnd	Sick	Wnd	
3rd Coldstream Gds.	.	.	2	-	To duty:-
1st Irish Gds.	.	.	.	4	1st Irish Gds - 1
1st K.R.R.	1	-	4	1	1st Herts - 1
1st Kings	.	.	.	-	R.A.M.C. - 1
7th -do-	.	1	2	-	P.S. (P. Fahern) - 1
1st Berks.	.	.	.	2	7th London - 5
R.A.M.C. att. 1st KRR	.	1	.	3	
5th Kings	.	.	1	1	
1st Herts	1	.	.	3	
Total	2	2	10	14	
Other Divisions:					
6th London Regt.	1	.	1	.	To Light Duty:-
7th -do-	.	.	8	.	1st Herts - 2
15th -do-	.	.	3	.	
19th -do-	1	.	.	.	
No 3 Mobile Vet. Sect.	.	.	1	.	
Total	2	.	13	.	

Evac'd by M.A.C.:
  Officers - 1
  Other Ranks - 15
Retd to Duty:
  Officers - 2
  Other Ranks - 7
Retd to Light duty:
  Other Ranks - 2

		Sick	Wnd
Admitted	Officers	4	2
"	Other Ranks	23	14
Evacuated	Officers	1	2
"	Other Ranks	19	5
Remaining	Officers	13	4
"	Other Ranks	23	26

Officers Admitted

1st K.R.R.	Lt. A.J. Austin-Cartmell	Neuralgia & Debility
6th London	2nd Lt. A.E. French	Inflam. of Tonsils
19th "	" P.S. Spokes	Influenza
1st Herts.	Capt. E. Longmore	Debility following Concussion
7th Kings	Lt. W. Leslie Pattenbrigh	B.W. Lumbar
5th "	Lt. H.G. Keet	- R. arm

A.D.M.S.
2nd Div. 9 am
25/4/15

P.A. Lloyd Jones
Capt. R.A.M.C.
OC No 4 Field Amb

No 4 Field Ambulance.

Evacuation Returns 9 am.

Officers   Nil
Other Ranks.   Lying - 5
             Sitting - 2.

P. H. Lloyd Jones.

O.C. No 7 Motor Convoy
25/4/15.

Capt. R. Aml
OC No 4 Fld Amb

No 4 Field Ambulance.

Evacuation Return 3/pm

Officers :- 2

Other Ranks Lying :- 4
            Sitting :- 4

O.C. No 4 Motor Convoy
25-4-15

P.R Dyd.
for Capt R.A.M.C
O.C. No 4 Field Ambl.

Army Form C. 2118.

WAR DIARY
or
INTELLIGENCE SUMMARY.
(Erase heading not required.)

Instructions regarding War Diaries and Intelligence Summaries are contained in F.S. Regs., Part II. and the Staff Manual respectively. Title pages will be prepared in manuscript.

Hour, Date, Place	Summary of Events and Information	Remarks and references to Appendices
26th April, 1915 BETHUNE.	The following is a copy of an order issued to OC Reserve Sub-Division, No 4. to Ambae. No.1 Return all the men at once that were sent to you yesterday that you do not wish to employ at BEUVRY. No.2 Return No 3089 Pte Clerk J at once No.3 I am of opinion that if you do not post a Watches officer upon the Château now, you will lose J. The A.P.M. has given explicit instructions that sentries be kept on the premises with me at bedroom yesterday evening that he would on no account allow N.C.O's or men to sleep in the house. No.4. No medical officers can be spared from here. No.5. An officer must inspect the Château and School at BEUVRY once daily." The following is the reply from the OC. Reserve Sub-Division:— No.1 Complied with. No.2 Complied with. Nos. 3, 4 & 5. Will I am in charge of No.1 Harley Street and PONT FIXE a Sapper dressing Station & am also M.O. to stop in BEUVRY. To send a M.O. daily to BEUVRY	[signature]

(73989) W4141—463. 400,000. 9/14. H.&J.Ltd. Forms/C. 2118/10.

Army Form C. 2118.

WAR DIARY
or
INTELLIGENCE SUMMARY
(Erase heading not required.)

Hour, Date, Place	Summary of Events and Information	Remarks and references to Appendices
26th April, 1915. BETHUNE. (Continued)	Number of Casualties - 39. Lieut H. Elliot, 1st Kings Regt. admitted to main dressing Station suffering from Shrapnel shot Wound. He was successfully operated upon. 2nd Lt. F. Brown, 4th Seaforths, (G.S.W. Shoulder) Capt. J. Y. Townes, 58th Rifles, (G.S.W. Head) } Evac'd Lieut M. L. Pillersdorph, (G.S.W. Back) } by No 7 " N. G. Kent, 5th Kings, (G.S.W. Arm) } M.A.C. " F. K. M. Thomson, on list 21th Lancer. (Newwier) Capt Nicoll, 3rd Sussex. (Neuralgia) Lieut T. W. Waldraugh, 6th London 2nd Lt. J. G. Gregory, 6th London } Returned Chaplain Rev. H. F. A. Glennon, 2nd Munsters } to Duty.	OKD

No. 4 Field Ambulance.

No. of sick wounded by Units admitted during 24 hours ended 9.0am 25/4/15.

Units 2nd Div.	Officers		Other Ranks		Remarks
	Sick	Wounded	Sick	Wounded	
2nd Grenadier Gds.	.	.	1	.	
1st Irish Gds.	1	.	1	7	To Duty:-
3rd Coldstream Gds.	.	.	1	.	2nd H.L.I. - 1
2nd — do —	.	.	.	1	self inflicted case
2nd South Staffs.	.	.	2	.	
15th Bat'y. R.F.A.	.	.	1	.	
2nd L. Att. R.F.A.	.	.	1	.	
2nd Ox & Bucks	.	.	1	.	
M.M.G.S. 1st Bat'y.	.	.	1	.	
A.C.C.	.	.	1	.	
A.G.A. 26th H.Bty.	.	.	1	.	
1st Herts.	1	.	.	.	
1st R. Berks	.	.	3	.	
50th Bat'y. R.F.A.	.	.	1	.	
1st K.R.R.	.	.	.	1	
R.E. (170th Coy. 5von).	.	1	.	.	
R.A. (2nd Div)	1	.	.	.	
R.G.A. 35th H.Bty.	1	.	.	.	
2nd Worcesters.	.	.	.	1	
R.F.A.H. Bat'y.	.	.	.	1	
Total.	4	1	14	13	
Other Divisions.					To Light duty:-
K.O.Y.L.I. attd. R.E.(170Coy).	.	1	.	.	11th Coy R.E - 1
18th London Regt.	1	.	.	.	2nd Sth. Staff - 1
HQ. 2nd. Staff. London Div.	.	.	.	1	8th London - 1
					31st Coy. R.E - 1
Total	1	1	.	1	

Evac. by M.A.C:-
Officers - 4
Other Ranks - 16
Retd to Duty:-
Officers -
Other Ranks - 1
Retd to Light Duty
Other Ranks - 4

	Sick	Wounded
Admitted Officers	5	2
" Other Ranks	14	14
Evacuated Officers	4	.
" Other Ranks	12	9
Remaining Officers	14	6
" Other Ranks	25	31

Officers Admitted

Unit	Name	Condition
1st Herts.	Lt. R.G. BORWICK	Debility following Concussion.
R.A. 2nd Div.	Lt. G.L. KAYE	Periostitis femoris.
35th H.Bty. R.G.A	Lt. A.V. ROBERTSON	Neurasthenia
attd Irish Gds.	Chaplain Rev. Father GWYNN	Lumbago.
HQ. Gen'l. Staff. London Div.	Capt. G.H. CHUBB	Neurasthenia
K.O.Y.L.I. attd R.E.(170Coy)	Capt. F.H. BOARDALL	Toxaemia Gas poisoning
170th Coy. R.E.	2nd Lt. H.D. MARTIN	— do —

P. A. Lloyd Jones
Capt. R. AMC.
OC No. 4 Field Amb.

A.D.M.S.
2nd Div. 26/4/15.

No 4 Field Ambulance.

Evacuation Return

Officers — Sitting · 1
Other Ranks — Lying · 6

G J Dyne
Capt. R. AMC
O.C. No 4 Field Amb.

O.C. No 7. M.A.C.
28-4-15

No 4 Field Ambulance.

Evacuation Return 3 pm

Officers 4 { 3 Lying
               1 Sitting

Other Ranks. Lying 4
             Sitting 5

O.C. No 4 Motor Convoy
26 4 15

for Capt R H McC
O.C. No 4 Field Amb

Army Form C. 2118.

WAR DIARY
or
INTELLIGENCE SUMMARY.
(Erase heading not required.)

Instructions regarding War Diaries and Intelligence Summaries are contained in F.S. Regs., Part II. and the Staff Manual respectively. Title pages will be prepared in manuscript.

Hour, Date, Place	Summary of Events and Information	Remarks and references to Appendices
26th April, 1915 BETHUNE. (Continued)	will entail the use of an extra car — I assume you propose supplying this, and don't expect me to use the cars here at present as these in my opinion are inadequate for the higher service of Division. BEUVRY is 4 miles from me which means that I am without a M.O. for nearly 1½ hours every day if I am to carry out this inspection." Car sent daily at 10 a.m.	

WAR DIARY
or
INTELLIGENCE SUMMARY.

Army Form C. 2118.

Hour, Date, Place	Summary of Events and Information	Remarks and references to Appendices
27th April, 1915 BETHUNE.	Number of Casualties - 47 Colonel Mr Tomlin 2/og London Regs was admitted to Officer Dressing Station suffering from Shell-shock. Capt. A Deane-Radcliffe, ad 19th Battn'io. (G.S.W. Chest) Major the Hon. C.N.B. Willoughby, M.P., 1st Coldm Gds. (Influenza) 2nd Lt. P.S. Spokes, 19th London (Influenza) Lieut N.I. Roberts (R.G.A.) (Neurasthenia) " R.S. Walley, 2nd K.R.R. (Shell wd Nose & knee) " C.L. Clairmont, 2nd K.R.R. (" - Hand) Evacuated by No 7 M.A.C. 2nd Lt. C.A.C. Rowley, 23rd London } Returned to duty " A.W. Williamson, R.E. } " H.B. Martin, R.E.	

No. 4 Field Ambulance.

No. of sick & wounded, by Units, admitted during 24 hours ended 9.0 am 27-4-15.

Units – 2nd Div.	Officers		Other Ranks		Remarks
	Sick	Wonded	Sick	Wonded	
1st Irish Gds.	.	.	2	.	To Duty:
3rd Colds. Gds.	.	.	3	8	
2nd do	.	.	2	1	Officers:
2nd South Staffs	.	.	1	.	
M.M.G. Sect. 1st Bde.	.	.	1	.	6th London – 2
5th Kings	.	.	3	.	2nd Munsters – 1
~~R.G.A. (4th H.Bty)~~					
R.E. (170th Coy).	.	.	1	.	Other Ranks
1st E.A. R.E.	.	.	3	.	Nil.
1st Kings	1	.	.	.	
A.C.C.	.	.	1	.	
7th Kings	.	.	.	1	
A.S.C. 2nd Div. Supply Col.	1	.	.	.	
3rd K.R.R.	.	2	.	.	
Total	2	2	17	10	
Other Divisions					To Light Duty:
R.F.A. 26th H.Bty	.	.	1	.	
58th Rifles	.	1	1	.	R.E. 21st Coy – 1
4th Seaforth Hldrs.	.	1	.	.	
23rd London Regt.	.	.	.	1	R.F.A. 16th Bty – 1
R.G.A. (6th Bty Trench Mortars)	.	.	.	1	
1st Kings Lancaster Regt.					6th London – 1
attch 1st L.N. Lancs	1	.	.	.	
3rd Sussex	1	.	.	.	
17th London	.	.	.	.	
Total	2	2	1	2	

Prevailing disease – Nil
No. admitted with Foot troubles – Nil

Evac'd by M.A.C.				Sick	Wond.
Officers – 7	Admitted	Officers		5	4
Other Ranks – 16	-"-	Other Ranks		18	12
Rett to Duty:	Evacuated	Officers		6	4
Officers – 3					
Other Ranks – –	-"-	Other Ranks		10	9
Rett to Light Duty:	Remaining	Officers		13	6
Other Ranks – 3.	-"-	Other Ranks		33	34

Officers admitted

4th Seaforths Hldrs.	2nd Lt. T. BROWN	G. Tw. Shoulder
58th Rifles	Capt. T.Y. TANCRED	Head
1st Kings Lancaster attch 1st L.N. Lancs.	Lt. F.K.M. THOMAS	Neuritis
3rd Sussex	Capt F.A.B. NICOLL	Supraorbital Neuralgia
A.S.C. 2nd Supply Colm.	Lt. V.D.R. CONLAN	Contused L. Shoulder.
1st Kings	Lt. M. ELLIOT	Strangulated Hernia
2nd K.R.R	2Lt. G.S. WALLEY	Shell Wd Nose & Sinus
-do-	2Lt. C.L. CLAREMONT	-"- wrist
17th London	2nd Lt. F.V. CROFT	Anaphy...

A.D.M.S. 27/4/15.
2 Div
Capt. R. ame
O.C. No 4 Field Ambulance

No 4 Field Ambulance
" "

Evacuation Return 9 am.
" "

Other Ranks Lying: 2
             Sitting: 3

O.C. No 4 Motor Convoy
27. 4. 15

G E Dupe
Capt R.A.M.C.
for O.C. No 4 Fd Ambl.

No 4 Field Ambulance.

Evacuation Return 3 pm

Officers 7   3 Lying
              4 Sitting

Other Ranks Lying #5.
            Sitting. 13

O.C. No 4 Motor Convoy
24-4-15

GK Dyas

Capt R.A.M.C

Army Form C. 2118.

WAR DIARY
or
INTELLIGENCE SUMMARY.
(Erase heading not required.)

Hour, Date, Place	Summary of Events and Information	Remarks and references to Appendices
28th April, 1915 BETHUNE	The following is a copy of an order issued to the Bearer Sub-Division, No. 4 to Ambce. "Under instructions from A.D.M.S. 2nd Division No. 13/50 dt. 28/4/15. One complete Section No. 5 Field Ambulance will take over Advanced Dressing Station, BEUVRY, from the detachment of No. 4 Field Ambulance at 10 a.m., 29th instant."	

Army Form C. 2118.

WAR DIARY
or
INTELLIGENCE SUMMARY.
(Erase heading not required.)

Hour, Date, Place	Summary of Events and Information	Remarks and references to Appendices
29th April 1915 BETHUNE	Number of Casualties = 57. Colonel McTomlin, 21st London (Concussion) Capt A. E. Brown, Royal (Neuralgia) " J. L. Ruffer, 4th Bn Watch (Bomb wrist Foot) ⎫ Lieut C. A. Baker, 1st S.W.B. (Influenza) ⎬ Evac'd " A. L. Palmer, 24th London (Neurasthenia) ⎪ by No.7 2nd Lt J. Pinder, 4th Seaforths (Wound Scalp) ⎪ M.A.C. Lieut M. D. Downes, 2nd R. Sussex (G.S.W. Buttock) ⎪ 2nd Lt F. W. Croft, 17th London (Paraphimosis) ⎭ 2nd Lt R.S. French, 6th London, returned to duty. No. 3387 Pte E Spencer, R.A.M.C. (No.4 to Ambce transferred) to Base Hospital suffering from Influenza	(PMS)

No 4 Field Ambulance

No. of sick & wounded, by Units, admitted during 24 hours ended 9 a.m. 28/4/15.

Units - 2nd Div.	Officers Sick	Officers Wnd'd	Other Ranks Sick	Other Ranks Wnd'd	Remarks
3rd Coldstream Gds.				7	To Duty:- (Light)
2nd Grenadier Gds.			4	2	1st Irish Gds. - 3
1st Irish Gds.			2	.	3rd Colds. Gds. - 1
A.C.C.			1	.	5th Kings - 1
R.F.A 2 D.A.C.			1	.	65th Bty R.F.A - 1
R.F.A 16 Bty			1	.	1st K.R.R. - 2
7th Kings			2	2	R.F.A 2 DAC - 1
5th "			1	.	7th City of London - 5
2nd South Staffs.			1	.	8th -do- - 1
9th Kings			.	1	15th -do- - 3
1st R. Berks			3	.	Officers R. duty
R.F.A 70th Bty			1	.	R.E. 170th Coy - 2
R.E. 51st H.Q. Coy			1	.	23rd London - 1
2nd South Staffs attch R.E. 170th Coy			1	.	
2nd A.S.C.			.	1	
8th Kings	1	.	.	.	
Total	1	.	19	13	
Other Divisions:					
R.G.A 6th Bty Fred Mortar			.	1	To Duty:-
23rd London Regt			.	1	2 Worcesters - 1
A.S.C. H.Q. 2nd London Train			1	.	3 Colds Gds - 2
2nd Divs. London Cyclist			1	.	1st K.R.R.S - 3
R.F.A. 9th Bty			1	.	1 · Irish - 3
R.E. 170th Bty			.	2	
4th Black Watch		1	.	.	
4th Seaforth Iodrs.	1	1	.	.	
3rd London Regt.		1	.	.	
21st -do-		1	.	.	
5th R. Sussex		1	.	.	
2nd Field Amb. R. Amc.		.	.	.	
Belgian Car Fallel Armoured Train ?			1	.	
Total	1	5	4	4	

Prevailing disease - Caries Dentine
N° admitted with foot trouble - 1.

Evac'd by M.A.C:-
Officers - 7
Other Ranks - 24
Ret'd to Duty:-
Officers - 3
Other Ranks -
Ret'd to Light Duty:-
Other Ranks - 18

		Sick	Wnd'd
Admitted	Officers	6	1
"	Other Ranks	23	17
Evac'd	Officers	4	5
"	Other Ranks	27	23
Remaining	Officers	15	2
"	Other Ranks	29	28

P. A. Lloyd Jones
Capt. R. Amc.
Ot. N° 4 Field Amb.

A.D.M.S.
2nd Div. 28/4/15.

No. 4 Field Ambulance.

Evacuation Return 9. am.

Officers Sitting - 1.
Other Ranks. Lying - |||| |||| 5
            Sitting - |||| |||| || 12.

OC. No. 4 F.A.   Capt. R.A.M.C.
9. am.   OC No. 4 Field Amb
28/4/15.

No 4 Field Ambulance

Evacuation Return. 3pm

Officers Lying 1
Sitting 4 (4 Servants)

Other Ranks Lying. 3
Sitting. 4.

O.C. No 4 Motor Convoy. } Malcockcroft Lieut-Ram
28.4.15 } for Capt R.A.M.C,
} O.C. No 4 Field Ambl.

Army Form C. 2118.

WAR DIARY
or
INTELLIGENCE SUMMARY.
(Erase heading not required.)

Instructions regarding War Diaries and Intelligence Summaries are contained in F.S. Regs., Part II. and the Staff Manual respectively. Title pages will be prepared in manuscript.

Hour, Date, Place	Summary of Events and Information	Remarks and references to Appendices
29th April, 1915. BETHUNE.	The Schools and Chateau at BEUVRY were handed over to No. 5 Field Ambulance at 10 a.m. This morning Sir Manet Hennighan, Consulting Physician to the Forces visited the Dressing Station. Number of Casualties – 48 Capt. F.H. Ronsdall, att R.E. (Toxaemia - Gas Poisoning) Rev'd. R.V.F. Johnstone, 2nd Monco. (Abcess Neck) Revd C.J Sanders, 24th City of London (Synovitis) Evacuated by No. 7 M.A.C. 	

No. 4 Field Ambulance

No. of sick & wounded, by Units, admitted during 24 hours ended 9 am 29/4/15.

Units - 2nd Div.	Officers Sick	Officers Wound	Other Ranks Sick	Other Ranks Wound	Remarks
1st Grnr. Gds.	.	.	3	2	To Duty:-
2nd Grenadier Gds.	.	.	3	1	2nd Coldm. Gds. - 1
2nd Coldstream Gds.	.	.	1	1	R.F.A. 36 Bde - 1
3rd -do-	.	.	5	.	" 15 Bty - 1
1st R. Berks.	.	.	.	5	R.F.A. - 1
7th Kings	.	.	.	6	2nd Worcesters - 1
1st K.R.R.	.	.	.	1	M.G.S. - 1
2. Ox & Bucks	.	.	3	1	H.F.A. 15th Bty - 1
A.C.C.	.	.	1	.	
2nd South Staffs	.	.	1	.	
5th Kings	.	.	.	1	
1st Kings	.	.	2	.	
2nd H.L.I.	.	.	2	.	
R.E. 11th Field Coy.	.	.	1	.	
R.F.C.	.	.	1	.	
R.F.A. 41st Bde A.C.	.	.	1	.	
Total			23	18	
Other Divisions					To Light Duty:-
23rd London Regt.	.	.	.	1	3rd Coldm. Gds. - 2
7/8th London -do- R.F.A.	.	1	1	.	1st Grnr. Gds. - 1
R.E. 1st Field Coy.	.	.	2	.	1st R. Berks - 3
R.E. 170th Coy.	.	.	1	.	5th Hvy R.F.A. - 1
1st Camerons	.	.	1	.	
22nd London Regt.	.	.	.	2	
24th -do-	.	1	1	.	
2nd R. Sussex	.	1	.	.	
3rd London Regt.	.	1	.	.	
1st Loyal N. Lancs	.	.	1	.	
4th Siege Bty. R.G.A.	1	.	.	.	
Total	2	4	6	4	

Evac'd by M.A.C.:
Officers - 8
Other Ranks - 31

Ret'd to Duty:-
Officers - 1
Other Ranks - 7

Ret'd to Light Duty:-
Other Ranks - 7

	Sick	Wound
Admitted Officers	2	4
Other Ranks	28	22
Evacuated Officers	7	2
Other Ranks	21	24
Remaining Officers	10	3
Other Ranks	36	26

Officers admitted

2nd R. Sussex — Lt. W.D. Downes — G.S.W. L. Buttock
3rd London Regt. — 2 Lt. G.C. Pulman — G.S.W. abdomen
1/4 N. Lancs — Capt. G.N. Hay — Enteritis
4th Siege Bty R.F.A. — A.G. Russell — Inflam of Pharynx
24th London Regt. — 2 Lt. G. Davies — B.W. L. Hand & Side
2nd -do- — F.N. Parker — B.W. Head

P.A. Lloyd Jones
Capt. R.A.M.C.
I/C No. 4 Field Amb.

ADMS.
2nd Div. 29/4/15.

No 4 Field Ambulance.

Evacuation Return.

Officers. - Sitting - 1.

Other Ranks - Sitting - 3.
     Lying - 3.

O.C. No 7 M.A.C.
9 a.m. 29/4/18.

M Cockeroft Lt RAMC
for Capt R. AMC
O.C. No 4 Field Amb.

No 4 Field Ambulance.

Evacuation Return 3pm.

Officers. Sitting 2   (2 Servants)

Other Ranks Lying 1
              Sitting 8

O.C. Noy Motor Convoy 3   G.T.Dyke
29-4-15   Capt R.A.M.C
                           O.C. No 4 Fd. Amb.

Army Form C. 2118.

WAR DIARY
or
INTELLIGENCE SUMMARY.
(Erase heading not required.)

Instructions regarding War Diaries and Intelligence Summaries are contained in F. S. Regs., Part II. and the Staff Manual respectively. Title pages will be prepared in manuscript.

Hour, Date, Place	Summary of Events and Information	Remarks and references to Appendices
30th April, 1915 BETHUNE.	Lieut A.J. Andrews, R.A.M.C. joined the Unit today from No 6 General Hospital, Rouen, for duty. Number of Casualties - 37 Lieut. H.L. King, 1st Kings, Malaria. 2nd Lt. G.C. Pulman, 3rd London, G.S.W. Abdomen } Died Lieut C.R. Mancripe, 1st Notts & Derby, S7 M.A.C. } by no.	

No. 4 Field Ambulance.

No. of Sick & wounded admitted, by Units, during 24 hours ended 9. am 30/4/15.

Units - 2nd Div	Officers		Other Ranks		Remarks
	Sick	Wondd	Sick	Wondd	
1st. Irish Gds.	.	.	.	2	To Duty:-
2nd Grenadier Gds.	.	.	3	4	M.M.P. - 1
5th. King's	.	.	8	.	1st. Irish Gds - 1
2nd South Staff.	.	.	4	1	
A.C.C.	.	.	1	.	
1st. K.R.R.	.	.	1	.	
1st. R. Berks.	.	.	.	1	
1st. King's	.	.	1	.	
47th. Bty R.F.A.	.	.	1	.	
A.S.C. 2 Div. Train	.	.	1	.	
Total	.	.	23	8	
Other Divisions					
R.F.A. 14th B. Dak	.	.	1	.	To Light Duty:-
-"- 115th Bty	.	.	.	2	3rd Colds. Gds - 1
24th London Regt.	.	.	.	1	2nd -do- - 1
1st Northants.	.	1	.	.	1st Irish Gds - 1
2nd. K.R.R.	.	1	.	.	R.E. (170th Coy) - 1
Total	.	2	2	3	

Prevailing disease - Sprain Ankle
No. admitted with Foot troubles - 1.

Evacd by M.A.C.:-
OFFICERS - 3
OTHER RANKS - 20
Retd to Duty:-
OFFICERS - Nil
OTHER RANKS - 3
Retd to Light Duty
OTHER RANKS - 4

		Sick	Wondd
Admitted	Officers	.	2
-"-	Other Ranks	25	11
Evacuated	Officers	3	1
-"-	Other Ranks	16	10
Remaining	Officers	.	4
-"-	Other Ranks	45	27

Officers Admitted

1st. Northants. - Lieut C.L. WAUCHOPE Shell wnd R. Leg.
2nd K.R.R. -"- R.C. FEATHERSTONHAUGH -"- L. Arm & L. Leg.

P.A. Lloyd Jones
Capt. R.A.M.C.
O.C. No. 4 Field Amb.

A.D.M.S.
2nd Div. 9 am 30/4/15

No 4 Field Ambulance.

Evacuation Return

Officers - Nil

Other Ranks.   Sitting - 1
              Lying - 4.

                                    Basil M Murphy
                                    Lt. Capt. R.Am.C.
O.C. No 7 M.AC.   O.C. No 4 Field Amb
9. am 30/4/18.

No 4 Field Ambulance

Evacuation Return 3/pm.

Officers Lying 2
Sitting 1   (3 Servants).

Other Ranks Lying. 8.
Sitting. 11

O.C. No 4 Motor Convoy
30.4.15

R Boyd
Capt R.A.M.C.
O.C. No 4 Fd Amb.

List of operations performed.

Lt. Elliot   1. King's   Strangulated Hernia ⎱ 26.4.1915
~~Lt. Reade~~   ~~Seaforths~~   & Hydrocele of cord. ⎰

2Lt. J.N Croft   17 London Rgt.   Paraphimosis   ⎫
Capt J.L. Rettie   4 Black Watch.   Bomb wd. face   ⎬ 27.4.1915
Pte J. Jackson   1 Royal Berks.   Appendicitis   ⎭

                                       Basil L Murphy.
                                         Lt RAMC.

April 1st – 30th
Operations.

(1) For GSW Skull and Brain — 5 Cases
(2) For GSW Abdomen — 3 Cases
(3) For Acute Appendicitis — 3 Cases
(4) For Strangulated Hernia — 1 Cases

www.ingramcontent.com/pod-product-compliance
Lightning Source LLC
Chambersburg PA
CBHW081434160426
43193CB00013B/2274